Jaime J. Sucher

Shetland Sheepdogs

Everything about Purchase, Care,
Nutrition, Breeding, and Diseases

With a Special Chapter on
Understanding Shetland Sheepdogs

With 35 Drawings and 20 Color Photographs

Consulting Editor: Matthew M. Vriends, PhD

New York • London • Toronto • Sydney

All inquiries should be addressed to:
Barron's Educational Series, Inc.
250 Wireless Boulevard
Hauppauge, New York 11788

Library of Congress Catalog Card No. 89-38592

International Standard Book No. 0-8120-4264-6

Library of Congress Cataloging in Publication Data

Sucher, Jaime J.
    Shetland sheepdogs: everything about purchase, care nutrition breeding, and diseases: with a special chapter on understanding Shetland sheepdogs: with color photographs by well-known photographers and drawings by Michele Earle-Bridges / Jaime J. Sucher: consulting editor. Matthew M. Vriends/
            p.   cm.
    ISBN 0-8120-4264-6
    1. Shetland sheepdog.   I. Vriends, Matthew M., 1937-   . II. Title.
    SF429.S62S83   1990   89-38592
    636.7'37—dc20   CIP

About the Author: Jaime J. Sucher, is Director of Research and Development for a manufacter of pet products. He is the author of numerous articles on pet nutrition and *Golden Retrievers* (Barron's).

Photo Credits:
Michele Earle-Bridges: pages 10 top and bottom left, 27, 28, 45 bottom right, 63bottom, 64; backcover. William van Vught: front cover; inside front cover; pages 9, 10 bottom right, 45 top and bottom left, 46, 63 top; inside back cover; back cover.

Illustrations:
Michele Earle-Bridges.

Advice and Warning:
This book is concerned with selecting, keeping, and raising Shetland sheepdogs. The publisher and the author think it is important to point out that the advice and information for Shetland sheepdog maintenance applies to healthy, normally developed animals. Anyone who acquires an adult dog or one from an animal shelter must consider that the animal may have behavioral problems and may, for example, bite without any visible provocation. Such anxiety-biters are dangerous for the owner as well as the general public.
    Caution is further advised in the association of children with dogs, in meetings with other dogs, and in exercising the dog without a leash.

Printed and Bound in Hong Kong

0123 4900 98765432

Contents

Contents

Preface

There is little wonder that the Shetland sheepdog (widely called the *Sheltie*) is quickly becoming one of the most popular dog breeds. Besides being a beautiful, intelligent, and devoted pet, its small size makes it ideal for people of most walks of life. The modern Sheltie is equally suited for life on the farm as well as in a city apartment.

The Shetland sheepdog possesses all the traits associated with herding dogs. They are obedient, loyal, and quick to learn. In the field they prove to be extremely hearty, rugged little dogs, with great agility and grace. Shelties rarely shy away from strangers, although they are usually wary of them. A member of this breed is very protective of its flock or "family." Thus, the Sheltie makes an ideal watchdog.

The long, thick coat of the Sheltie proved extremely valuable to the breed in their ancestral home of the Shetland Islands. These islands, off the northern coast of Scotland, are frequented by harsh storms, and have an environment where only the smallest and most durable animals can survive.

While the physical characteristics of the Shetland sheepdog are the result of careful breeding practices and environmental influences, the temperament of the breed also reflects generations of shepherd-sheepdog relationships. Few breeds can match the devotion and gentle nature that a Sheltie shows to its human family.

I have often wondered why it has taken so long for the Shetland sheepdog to reach its recent popularity. Besides the aforementioned traits, the Shetland sheepdog is easy to groom, suffers from few genetic diseases, and is equally suited to outdoor and indoor life.

If you have chosen to get a Sheltie, or are considering owning one, this practical manual will tell you everything you need to know about choosing and raising Shetland sheepdogs. It will answer your questions about keeping a dog in your house or in a kennel. Detailed instructions tell you how to help the dog adapt to its new home and how to feed and care for it. This manual also provides information about preventive medicine, symptoms of illness, and treatment of various injuries and diseases.

There is also a chapter devoted entirely to training your Shetland sheepdog. For novice dog owners, here are the fundamentals of instruction to develop a sound program for daily practice sessions. Experienced owners may also find new ideas to incorporate into their daily regimen.

A final chapter traces the breed's origin and history, describes the basic behavior patterns of Shelties, as well as dogs in general, and outlines the breed standard.

I would like to acknowledge the assistance of Matthew Vriends, PhD, consulting editor of this series and Helgard Niewisch, DVM, who read the manuscript and made many valuable suggestions.

Jaime J. Sucher

Should You Buy a Sheltie?

Making an Intelligent Choice

The Shetland sheepdog, or Sheltie, has often mis-leadingly been referred to as a miniature collie, im-plying that the Sheltie was established by inbreed-ing smaller collies to obtain the diminutive stature that characterizes the breed. In reality, however, it is believed both the Shetland sheepdog and the collie are descended from the same ancestor. One line evolved into a larger breed; the other, into a smaller one. This common ancestor is believed to be the Border collie, which can still be found today herding sheep in the Scottish highlands.

In addition to selective breeding, the resulting smaller size of the Sheltie was due to the environ-ment of the Shetland Islands where the breed orig-inated. The Shetlands, a small chain of islands along the northern coast of Scotland, have a rocky terrain and sparse vegetation, and are frequented by severe storms. The harshness of landscape and weather has led to a perennial scarcity of food, thereby put-ting a premium on small, sturdy domesticated an-imals. In fact, most of the animals that are found in the Shetlands seem to have shrunk from larger relatives into miniature forms. Besides the Sheltie, these islands are home to the well-known Shetland pony. Shetland sheep and cattle are also of lilli-putian size.

The diminutive size of the Shetland sheepdog is one reason it is quickly becoming one of the most popular purebred dogs in America. A smaller dog has little problem adjusting to the confined spaces of an apartment, yet the Sheltie's courage, loyalty, obedience, and herding ability make it an excellent dog for the farm as well.

As the name implies, the Shetland sheepdog was originally bred to tend sheep. In order to be suc-cessful in this endeavor, the Sheltie had to be loyal, obedient, and courageous. A sheepdog had to pro-tect its flock from danger, yet not frighten the herd itself. In addition, the sheepdog had to be hardy, independent, and able to protect itself from its harsh surroundings. The Shetland sheepdog was bred to achieve the temperament needed for the job, and its thick coat gives ample protection from the weather. Through years of selective breeding, these traits have become synonymous with the breed and can be found in all of today's Shelties.

Shetland sheepdogs make excellent house pets. They are fast learners and extremely obedient. They are small, beautiful, and easy to care for. They possess the perfect temperament to be with chil-dren and are equally suited to be a watchdog. All these traits make the Shetland sheepdog the ideal pet for a diverse range of people regardless of their living space or their age.

Whether to buy a Sheltie is an important deci-sion. Lack of awareness of the responsibility of dog ownership can result in an unhappy relationship for both the dog and the owner. Before you buy a Shet-land sheepdog, carefully consider the following:

- Do you have the time, energy, and patience to raise a dog properly?
- If you purchase a Sheltie puppy, would you be willing to change your schedule to meet the dog's needs? The needs of a puppy are quite different from those of an adult dog. Puppies are not inde-pendent and require more frequent feedings and closer supervision.
- Are you willing to devote some of your free time to the dog? Do you travel on weekends or take long vacations? Are you willing to travel only to areas where you can bring your Shetland sheepdog? Al-though dogs can withstand the stress of travel fairly well, they are prohibited in many hotels and motels.
- Do you understand the long-term commitment involved in owning a Shetland sheepdog? A dog should never be purchased impulsively, especially because a Sheltie may live a dozen years or more.
- Do you have a yard, or is there a park or wooded area where your dog can get its much-needed ex-ercise? The Shetland sheepdog is a small breed and can be comfortably housed even in a small apart-ment. However, Shelties are a working breed, and both their physical and mental welfare depend on getting sufficient exercise.

Should You Buy a Sheltie?

• Finally, can you afford to keep a Shetland sheepdog? Aside from the initial expenses of buying the dog and necessary supplies, feeding may cost as much as $40 per month. Additional expenses include annual visits to the veterinarian (see page 12).

Consider these questions carefully before you purchase a Shetland sheepdog. Free–ranging dogs constitute a major problem in the United States, as well as in many other countries. Studies indicate that this problem is due more to human irresponsibility than to a dog's following its wild instincts. In the long run, this situation can lead to the outbreak of diseases from nonvaccinated, homeless animals. These facts emphasize the importance of responsible pet ownership.

With all points considered, if you still wish to purchase a Sheltie, find out if there is in your area a chapter of the American Shetland Sheepdog Association, who can help answer your relevant questions.

Choosing a Male or a Female

Once you have decided to buy a Shetland sheepdog, you will have to choose either a male or female dog. In this breed there is little difference between the sexes. Both have about the same disposition and are of equal physical proportions. As with most breeds of dogs, the males are usually more likely to roam while the females tend to stay near home. With a Sheltie, the only time you might prefer a specific sex is if you are interested in breeding the dog. If you are considering a kennel housing, females are preferable.

If you select a female and have no intention of breeding her, have the dog spayed. Because there are an alarming number of homeless dogs in the United States, owners should take all possible precautions against the increase of unwanted animals. Spaying the female dog also avoids the messiness that will occur when she is "in heat." A spayed female will be more likely to avoid breast tumors,

ovarian cysts, false pregnancies, and other ailments.

Note, however, that if you plan to enter your female in a dog show, she will be disqualified if she is spayed.

Choosing an Adult or a Puppy

While the choice of gender in a Sheltie may not be important, whether you buy an adult or puppy certainly is. When making this choice, keep the following in mind.

One of the greatest rewards of owning a Shetland sheepdog is watching it grow from an unbelievably cute, awkward, tiny bundle of fur into a beautiful, dignified, loyal adult. However, this requires a great deal of patience, time and energy. A properly trained adult is the result of diligent attention by owners who gave their puppy understanding, love, and the needed thorough training. All too easily dog owners neglect their duties, and the result is a relationship in which neither the dog nor the owner is happy.

For the person who does not have the time to devote to a puppy, the selection of an adult Sheltie offers other advantages. A well–trained Shetland sheepdog makes a fine pet. Mature Shelties will usually have little trouble adapting to a new household, thereby saving the new owners the time needed to raise, train, and housebreak a puppy. An adult Sheltie, needing significantly less attention than a puppy, makes an ideal pet for the elderly or for a working family. The greatest drawback to buying an older Sheltie is that you may find it extremely difficult to correct bad habits the dog may have already acquired.

If you are interested in obtaining an adult Sheltie, start by contacting a reputable breeder. It may be possible for you to buy or even adopt a dog that is too old to be bred safely. By doing this, you can be sure of acquiring a Sheltie that was raised by a caring and knowledgeable person.

Should You Buy a Sheltie?

When choosing between a Sheltie puppy and an adult, keep in mind that raising a puppy will allow you to train it to the habits of your household. Adult dogs, on the other hand, need significantly less attention, which means less work, especially for an older owner.

If you are looking for a show dog, you have two options. First, you can purchase a potential show puppy from a reputable breeder and raise it yourself: this way you will have the satisfaction of knowing that you have done the job yourself. Alternatively, you can purchase a mature show dog: this way, you are assured of your Sheltie's quality and beauty.

Where and How to Buy a Shetland Sheepdog

The first step in purchasing a puppy is to contact the Secretary of the American Shetland Sheepdog Association or the American Kennel Club and get a list of reputable dealers and well–established, registered Sheltie breeders in your area. Visit as many pet stores and breeders in your area as possible.

Visit each store or kennel to inspect the dogs and the conditions in which they are kept. The time and effort you spend in finding the right Sheltie will save you trouble and heartache later on.

When visiting the kennels, keep in mind that the quality of your puppy will be a direct reflection of the quality of the breeder. Conscientious breeders will make every effort to satisfy you in order to maintain their reputation. Always feel free to ask the breeder questions, regardless of how silly they may seem. A good breeder will be able to answer all your relevant questions and be of invaluable help when it comes time to select your puppy.

The least emphasis should be put on the price of the puppy. Never be swayed into buying a dog because it is "cheap." The old adage, "You get what you pay for," is all too true when buying a dog. A bargain price may indicate the dog was raised strictly for profit by an inexperienced breeder, or that the dog is in poor health. A more expensive dog from an experienced and reputable breeder may save you a lot of future veterinarian bills.

You should also avoid Shelties from kennels not dedicated solely to breeding and raising Shetland sheepdogs. Breeders who raise several species of dogs are not always knowledgeable about the special needs of each breed.

As you visit each store or kennel on your list, pay special attention to the dogs' housing. Be sure the surroundings are clean and that the dogs have room to move about freely. Observe the coat conditions and overall appearance of all of the dogs. Each of these factors are indicators of the quality of the operation. Once you have found a dealer or breeder in whom you have confidence, you must then choose your puppy.

Selecting the Right Puppy for You

At first glance, Shetland sheepdog puppies look alike—adorable, tiny bundles of fur and wrinkles. Learn to see past this, and resist the impulse to buy the first puppy that catches your fancy (which is most likely the first puppy you see). As you observe the puppies, you will begin to notice subtle differences in their physical characteristics and their temperament. Though they may be only a few weeks old, these differences can be used to help you select the right puppy for you.

While all Sheltie puppies are cute and adorable, it will take many weeks before they begin to attain the physical attributes that characterize the breed.

Should You Buy a Sheltie?

Examine the puppy's coat; it should be smooth and shiny. Its eyes should be bright, and the puppy should be sturdily built. Shetland sheepdog puppies should look alert and be slightly cautious, for they are herding dogs. In most cases, it would be best to avoid both hyperactive and overly sedate dogs.

If you watch the puppies play together, you get an idea of their individual temperaments. Some may be bolder; others, more shy. The puppy's temperament is a good indicator of what the dog's adult behavior will be like, and you can therefore select a dog whose disposition will fit your home life.

Another good indicator of the puppy's temperament is its mother's behavior. After all, many of the puppy's behavioral characteristics are inherited from its sire (father) or dam (mother). Observe how the mother reacts to people. She should show no signs of fear and only the slightest amount of misgiving at the most. As herding dogs, Shelties are inherently protective. It may take a little time before the dam senses that you, a stranger, mean her and her litter no harm. This type of behavior is actually desirable in a watchdog; however, the dam should show no sign of aggression.

If the puppy appears to be in good health and of sound temperament, the next step is to check its pedigree papers. These papers are a written record of the dog's recent ancestry—a dog's family tree, with all the show champions in its lineage marked as such. In addition to this, the pedigree papers will show if the dog has had its eyes checked. Shetland sheepdogs, like many other breeds, may suffer from hereditary eye problems. When a breeder has the puppy's eyes checked and cleared, they are given a number that is placed on the pedigree. Never pur-

The alert and sometimes wary facial expressions that characterize Shelties can be seen in puppies as well as in adults.

chase a dog whose pedigree papers lack this number.

If the dog's pedigree is satisfactory, ask for the date the puppy was wormed, and be sure to get a written record of this to show your veterinarian. Do not be afraid to ask questions. A reputable dealer or breeder is as concerned with the puppy's welfare as you are. Also, do not be offended if a breeder asks questions about your experience with dogs and where you plan to raise your puppy. Take this as a sign of concern. In addition, keep an open line of communication so that the dealer or breeder can help you with any future problems.

How Much Will It Cost?

Though the initial purchase price of a Shetland sheepdog varies, expect to spend at least $200. Potential show dogs may sell for $1,000 or more. Generally, younger puppies will be less expensive than an older dog, because less time and money will have been invested in it.

There is nothing that compares to the varied expressions of Sheltie puppies. Here they can be seen at play, at rest, and learning new commands.

Food may cost as much as $30 or $40 a month, and you must also purchase equipment for feeding, grooming, and housing your dog. A dog requires annual immunizations against all infectious diseases, as well as an annual heartworm test (when you live in an area where this disease is endemic. See page 37.). Puppies and adult dogs may also have to be wormed. If you do not plan to breed your Sheltie, spaying or neutering is recommended. This will cost from $20 to $60. If your dog should get sick or injured, it may need additional, sometimes costly medical attention.

Finally, you will have to pay an annual licensing fee to your county or city, a fee to register your dog with the American Kennel Club, as well as annual dues if you join the American Shetland Sheepdog Association.

Since the long-term expenses of owning a Shetland sheepdog are much greater than the purchase price, carefully consider these costs before you decide to buy a dog.

When Can I Bring My Puppy Home?

Once you have selected the puppy that is best for you, you will have to arrange to take it home. The puppy should be seven weeks old when it moves to its new home. A puppy of this age should adapt very easily to its new environment, yet it should not be old enough to have picked up many bad habits. Recent studies have shown that during their eighth week, puppies become especially sensitive to environmental changes. If you cannot pick up the puppy during the seventh week, wait until the ninth week. Rather than risk behavior problems, wait until the puppy is ready for change.

If you select a Sheltie puppy from a local breeder, it is a good idea to visit your puppy several times before bringing it home. This will allow your puppy to get used to you and can help alleviate some of the stress that a newly separated puppy experiences.

Housing and Supplies

Indoor Space Requirements

I have previously mentioned that the diminutive size of the Shetland sheepdog offers many advantages when it comes to indoor space requirements. Logic dictates that a smaller dog requires a smaller space, and in this case, that is true. However, dogs are territorial animals, and although a Sheltie's "territory" does not need to be very large, it is important not to make it too small.

A Shetland sheepdog, whether an adult or a puppy, requires a quiet living area where it can feel comfortable and secure. Inside your home, you must provide your dog with a territory of its own— its regular eating and sleeping areas. In locating these areas, keep in mind that once established, these areas should not be moved. The dog will feel secure and protected only if it has a quiet, reliable place to rest undisturbed. This area should neither isolate the dog nor subject it to heavy human traffic.

Good resting areas are in corners where the dog is protected on two sides. These areas should also be draft-free and not in direct sunlight. The area should also make it easy to confine the dog's movements when you go to bed or when you leave the house. It is equally important that the Sheltie's sleeping area be at the right temperature. A puppy requires the temperature to be between 70° and 75°F (21°–24°C). This range is warm enough to help prevent the puppy from catching colds, and is not so warm as to make the dog sensitive to outside cold.

A Sheltie's sleeping area may be equipped with either a sleeping box and pad or a cage with a pad. This choice should be made in advance, depending on your method of housebreaking. (See the chapter entitled, "Basic and Advanced Training" page 59). I recommend using a cage, as it can also be invaluable for transporting and disciplining your puppy. Dogs are instinctively den animals, and the confined space will make a puppy feel safer and more comfortable than an open sleeping box.

The cage should be approximately 24 inches (61 cm) high, by 24 inches (61 cm) wide, by 30 inches (76 cm) long. It must have strong welds that cannot be broken by an active puppy.

The cage will be your puppy's "house" when you are not around to supervise. Some cages can also be used to carry your puppy when you go for a drive or to the veterinarian.

If you decide not to use a cage, purchase a sleeping box. Make sure it is large enough to accommodate a full–grown, spread–out dog. Line the box with cedar shavings and shredded newspapers and then place an old blanket over this layer. Your dog will find this very comfortable for sleeping.

If you are purchasing a sleeping box, it would be wise to avoid those made of wicker or other "soft" wood materials. These types of beds can be easily chewed apart by an active puppy. Likewise, if you decide to build your own box, use only non-splintering hardwoods. Because many stains and paints are toxic, leave the box unfinished.

When you are bringing home an unhousebroken puppy, it would be best not to give it an expensive pad. Puppies have little control over their bladder or bowels, so anything used in their bed should be either disposable or washable. In addition, be sure that anything you put in the bed is clean. Puppies are very susceptible to ailments, because their immune system is not fully developed, and their resistance to disease is low.

Like its sleeping place, a dog's feeding place should never be changed. Changes in sleeping and feeding places can cause your pet unnecessary stress. An animal under stress may exhibit behavioral changes as well as changes in many biological functions, including problems with digestion and excretion. It is best to place your dog's feeding area in an easily cleaned room, such as the kitchen.

Keeping Your Sheltie Outdoors

Unlike most toy and miniature breeds, the Shetland sheepdog is a rugged breed and may be kept outdoors—in most climates, all year round. However, it is advisable to bring your Sheltie indoors on cold winter nights.

If you decide your dog is to live outdoors, or if you leave your dog outside when you are not home, you must provide it with a fenced enclosure or run. The run should be at least 6 feet (2 m) wide, by 15 feet (5 m) long, by 6 feet (2 m) high, and it should be constructed of strong chain link fence. You can place partially buried boards around the bottom to prevent the dog from digging under the fence. The run can be as large as your yard. However, it should not be smaller than the size stated.

Use a few inches of smooth stone as a base. This will provide drainage when it rains, and it will prevent the dog from becoming muddy. Do not use concrete as a floor, because concrete will retain the smell of urine. The run must also provide your dog with some shade and shelter.

The best form of outdoor shelter is a doghouse. Whether you build your own or buy one, make sure it is raised several inches off the ground to avoid dampness and insects. The doghouse must be properly constructed to protect the dog against wind, rain, and cold, for even a minor draft can lead to serious respiratory ailments. The doghouse should be approximately 36 inches (91 cm) long, 30 inches (76 cm) high, and 30 inches (76 cm) wide. If the house is too small, the dog will not be able to stand or sleep comfortably. But do not make the house too large, because during cold weather the dog's body will provide the only form of heat. For this reason, it is also best to insulate the structure.

It is important to keep your Sheltie's house as clean as possible. When constructing a doghouse there are several things you can do to make cleaning easier. First, by hinging the roof, you can easily fold back the top of the doghouse to make the inside easily accessible. Next, you can line the floor of the structure with an easy to clean, waterproof material such as linoleum. You can also cover the linoleum with a thin layer of cedar shavings and over that you can place an old blanket. The cedar shavings will serve several purposes. They will help absorb excess moisture that may get into the house.

They will also make the floor more comfortable to sleep on. In addition, the natural oils in the cedar shavings will help repel fleas from your dog and the doghouse.

To prevent the inside of the house from being exposed to the cold winter winds, you should place the front opening so that it faces south. If you hang a piece of canvas or a blanket over the opening, making sure it overlaps sufficiently, you can help eliminate drafts. If you live in a climate where winter nights become very cold, you should find a place indoors where your dog can sleep.

Additional Equipment and Accessories

The first days after you bring your new puppy home are bound to be very busy and exciting. To avoid additional work or confusion, purchase the following items in advance and keep them available.

The most important pieces of equipment, at least from your growing Sheltie's point of view, are the food and water dishes. Both food and water dishes should be nonbreakable, heavy, and sturdy enough so that a Sheltie with a voracious appetite cannot tip them over. Plastic, stainless steel, and ceramic are all suitable materials. If you choose to use a ceramic bowl, however, be sure it was not fired with a lead–based glaze. Using bowls covered with these glazes, over a long period of time, can lead to lead poisoning.

During the life of your Sheltie, it may or may not be necessary to purchase more than one collar. Your puppy will require a light collar, but not necessarily a strong one. I recommend using either a leather or nylon collar that is adjustable to fit both a Sheltie puppy and an adult sheepdog. Bear in mind, though, that these collars deteriorate with age, and would therefore need to be replaced eventually. If your Sheltie is an adult, you may choose to use a chain collar, but be sure it is not too heavy or bulky for your dog. Another type of collar that you may want to purchase is a chain–choke collar, which can come in very handy when it is time to teach your dog the basic commands.

Leashes come in a wide variety of lengths and materials, and you may want to purchase more than one type. For regular walks, use a leash that is only a few feet long. This will enable you to quickly bring the dog to your side, should the need arise. It will also prevent your Sheltie from taking a destructive stroll through your neighbor's perfectly manicured garden. If you are lucky enough to possess a large yard, a 30–foot (10 m) leash, with an automatic reel, is useful. Because a Sheltie is not a large, strong dog, there is little need to get a leash made of anything stronger than leather or nylon. This is doubly true of Sheltie puppies. Sheltie puppies will chew, or attempt to chew, on anything that passes in front of their noses. Therefore you should never purchase a chain leash for your puppy. Chewing on the chain can damage a puppy's teeth.

A good safety device that you may want to purchase is reflecting tags or tape. The tags and tape attach to your dog's collar and leash, making both dog and owner more visible at night when headlights shine on them. This will make your nighttime walks much safer. You should also attach an identity tag, with your address and phone number, to the dog's collar. This simple and inexpensive precaution could prove to be invaluable, should your Sheltie ever become lost.

The owners of Shetland sheepdogs rarely need a muzzle for their dogs. However, you should keep one readily available in case of need. If you are planning on taking your Sheltie abroad, note that some foreign countries require all dogs to wear muzzles. A muzzle may also be necessary if your dog becomes seriously hurt and has to be taken to a veterinarian. A dog in severe pain may react unpredictably, so be prepared. When buying a muzzle, get one that can be adjusted for size. Remember that there is a big difference between the head of a Sheltie puppy and that of an adult dog.

Flea sprays, tweezers, and rubbing alcohol are

Should your dog become injured, and a muzzle not be available, you can use a necktie or a folded piece of cloth that is knotted in the center, tied under the chin, and finished off with a knot behind the neck. Tie this temporary muzzle firmly, *but not too tightly*.

helpful in case of external parasites. Flea sprays come in many forms, including aerosols, pump–on liquids, and alcohol–based liquids that you can rub on. Flea–control products also come in other forms such as foggers, powders, dips, and collars. Use tweezers to properly remove ticks, and rubbing alcohol to disinfect the wound.

Dog Toys

As with children, toys are an essential part of a dog's life, and are important to both its physical and mental well-being. Toys signify playtime. They let your puppy know that there is more to life than training sessions, eating, and sleeping. Playing with toys gives a dog exercise and allows a dog to work out frustration that it may be experiencing. In addition, toys allow a puppy to develop its survival instincts. If you watch your Sheltie playing with its toys you will see this for yourself. Watch your puppy get low to the ground and attempt to creep up on its target. Observe it studying its opponent, waiting until the time is right. Then watch it pounce and render its prey harmless. This entire act may take all of five seconds, but it is part of every puppy's instincts to survive. If all this is not enough to convince you of the importance of toys, I will give you one last reason to use them. Giving your puppy toys will spare your furniture, clothing, and other valued possessions from small, but well-defined teeth marks.

From the time a puppy begins to teethe it should always have a chewable toy to gnaw on. Rawhide bones are excellent chew-toys. They become soft enough so that they will not harm a young puppy's teeth, and at the same time will help strengthen your Sheltie's jaw muscles. Since a Sheltie puppy can quickly reduce a small rawhide bone to almost nothing, make sure to replace the bone before it becomes small enough for the puppy to swallow it whole. Avoid giving your dog any toy which it can shred and swallow, for this can cause choking or blockage of the digestive tract.

When choosing toys for your Sheltie, make sure they are designed for small dogs and are made of 100 percent nontoxic materials. Some forms of plastic are toxic, and many forms of wood can splinter. To be on the safe side never give your Sheltie any painted items. Some older types of paint contain lead, which may be harmful if swallowed in excess. Varnished toys are also potentially toxic and should be avoided.

Not all your Sheltie's toys need be store bought. Some of the best times my dogs have ever had were when we played "hide and seek" with some big cardboard boxes or shopping bags. Tennis balls are also among their favorite toys. If you decide to use a ball from around your house it should be of the proper size and material. Do not use golf balls or Ping-Pong balls, because they can be chewed upon and swallowed. Do not be afraid to use your imagination. There are many simple household items that you can use to keep your puppy entertained for hours.

Just remember to be selective in the items you give your puppy for toys. A Sheltie puppy will chew almost anything that will fit into its mouth. In addition, a mischievous Sheltie will tend to seek out anything with your scent, such as your old shoes and clothing. For this reason, keep these items out of your puppy's reach. Also, never give your puppy either your old slippers or toys that resemble valuable objects. To a Sheltie puppy, there is little difference between an old slipper and your new one. This is true of anything of value to you; letters, money, keys, and so on. Keep all valuable items away from your puppy, and you will prevent the development of bad habits.

Caring for a Shetland Sheepdog

Before the Puppy Comes Home

The first few days after a puppy is brought into its new home are usually hectic. It is therefore a good idea to prepare yourself and your house before bringing your puppy home. By taking a few steps in advance you can greatly reduce the confusion when y bring your puppy home.

Purc e beforehand all the necessary equipment and accessories, such as food and water dishes, collars, leashes, grooming supplies, etc. In addition, you should also choose the puppy's food (as recommended by the breeder), and purchase an adequate supply of it.

When you have bought all the supplies and have placed them in readily accessible locations, begin to "puppy-proof" your home. Remember that a young puppy is very curious, and as it roams through your house it will sniff, paw at, and chew almost everything. For this reason, place all potential hazards out of the puppy's reach.

Remove all poisons, including paints, cleaners, disinfectants, insecticides, and antifreeze. Store them in an area inaccessible to your puppy. Also, remove all sharp objects such as broken glass, nails, and staples. If you have an older home, make sure your dog does not eat paint chips containing lead.

Electrical wires must also be moved out of your puppy's reach. A dog chewing on electrical wires can be injured or killed by the resulting shock.

Finally, you should decide where the Sheltie's feeding and sleeping areas will be, and equip them accordingly. By doing all of these things, you can make the upcoming transition period much easier for both you and your puppy.

The First Days at Home

Most people find it difficult to adjust to a new environment. We undergo some emotional stress when we change jobs and are introduced to our new workmates, or meet the new neighbors when we move. We feel loneliness because we miss friends and loved ones. We are uncertain of what the future holds in this new place. We miss the security of everything we left behind.

A young puppy has much the same feelings the first days when it is home with you. You are taking it from the security of its mother and siblings, and placing it in an unfamiliar world, full of strange, new sights and sounds. The stress of this move makes your puppy's first few hours in your home very important. You now have an emotionally insecure, and very impressionable seven–week–old puppy in your home. You must make the transition period go as smoothly as possible. You must let your puppy know it is entering a calm, safe, and secure home. Assure your puppy that it need not fear, and it will be taken care of. Make your puppy's first day home a quiet one. Avoid having a horde of family and friends prodding your little friend before you can even get it in the door.

While it is advisable to avoid having the entire neighborhood stop by to pet and handle the puppy, it is a good idea to let it hear people moving around. The sound of its owner's footsteps, and an occasional confrontation between you and your puppy, will quickly wear away its feelings of loneliness and insecurity.

When your puppy arrives, it will probably want to urinate or defecate. Instead of entering your house, walk the puppy to a place you have chosen for its elimination area. Give the puppy about ten minutes to relieve itself, and then praise and pet it for doing so. This will help the puppy learn to defecate and urinate outdoors.

In order to help the puppy adjust, let it sniff around your home undisturbed. Then help it learn the location of its food and water dishes. Let your puppy continue to roam about, but do feel free to pet it and play with it. When it tires, pick it up and put it in its sleeping box or cage. Within a few days, the puppy should learn where its sleeping area is, and when tired, find its bed on its own.

To me, the next step in training your puppy is the hardest test you will face. Furthermore, it is

Caring for a Shetland Sheepdog

your first test, and failure here will mean greater problems in the future. Your puppy will probably whine, whimper, and wail, because it is in an unfamiliar place and because it misses its mother and siblings. It is important, however, that you remain firm. If the puppy sleeps in a cage, do not let it out. If you do, it will wail every time it wants to leave the cage. If you use a sleeping box, you might try to reassure the puppy by speaking softly, but do not take it from the box. Your puppy must learn to deal with loneliness as soon as possible.

By the time it is eight weeks old, a puppy should be fully weaned, and eating from a dish.

When feeding your puppy, you should follow a few fundamental rules. First, be sure to feed your puppy the same kind of food used by the breeder. Changes in surroundings will cause the puppy a certain amount of stress, which may affect its digestive system. By not changing its diet, you will avoid digestive problems. Second, try to feed your puppy on the same schedule used by the breeder. However, if that schedule is inconvenient, change the feeding times slowly to meet your schedule. Finally, never bother your dog while it is eating (or sleeping). A dog that is surprised may sometimes act unpredictably. Be sure also to explain this rule to your children.

If you must leave the house during your puppy's first few days, be sure it is not left alone. If no family member is available, ask a neighbor or a close friend to "puppy-sit." An unsupervised, curious puppy means only one thing—a mess.

Soon after your puppy arrives, you must begin to train it. Training will require time, energy, patience, understanding, and of course, love. From the minute your Sheltie arrives, begin to teach it its name. Other essential lessons are described in detail in the chapter, "Basic and Advanced Training" (page 59). Remember, the longer you wait to begin training, the harder it will be for your dog to learn.

Grooming a Shetland Sheepdog

The Shetland sheepdog is a long-haired breed, and as such requires a daily, vigorous brushing. Aside from this, the Sheltie will need additional grooming only periodically. It is best to begin handling and grooming your puppy as soon as possible so that it can become accustomed to the procedure. Whenever you are ready to begin, have your dog stand on a table or bench so that you do not have to bend down so much to work on it.

Equipment

You will need the following equipment to keep your Sheltie in top condition: a stiff bristle brush, a slicker brush, a comb, shears, nail clippers, and styptic powder.

Coat Care

A Sheltie's coat acts as a built-in air conditioning system, keeping the heat out during the sum-

A grooming table can be a tremendous help when brushing, combing, or trimming your Sheltie's coat.

mer, and the dog's body heat in during the winter. Therefore, coat care is important all year round.

Like most long-haired breeds, the Shetland sheepdog will shed mostly in the spring and fall. A dog that is kept indoors may tend to do some shedding all year round, and therefore, a daily brushing is required. Start by giving your dog a thorough brushing using a stiff bristle brush, followed by a slicker brush. By using a bristle brush first, you can untangle any snarls in the outer coat before you begin removing any of the shedding undercoat with the slicker brush.

Use the bristle brush to take care of the chest, the tail, the feathering on the legs, and the softer hair around the ears. Once these areas are brushed, you can quickly go over them with a comb to be sure that there is no matted hair. Any hair which becomes unusually long, straggly, or too matted to comb should be carefully removed using the shears.

The shape of a Sheltie's ears may vary somewhat, and as a result, there are differences in how they should be groomed. When the Sheltie assumes an attentive position, its ears should stand semi-erect, with just the tips folding forward. Unfortunately few Shelties can look like that without assistance. Some Shelties have low, houndlike ears, while others stand completely erect like that of a Great Dane. The amount of bend in the tip depends on the strength of a small muscle in the ear. If your Sheltie carries its ears low, like a hound, then you should trim off all extra hair around the tips of the ears. This will reduce the weight which pulls the ears down. Should your Sheltie have erect ears, then you may want to weigh them down. However, it is prudent to ask a breeder, veterinarian, or professional groomer about the weighting procedure. They can show you the method least irritating to your dog.

You should also trim the hair between the pads of your dog's feet. Cut this hair as short as possible. This will reduce the chance of infection in damp weather and will also improve the dog's traction.

While brushing, look for signs of external parasites such as fleas and ticks. If you see any, spray or powder the dog immediately. These parasites may be harder to eliminate if you leave them to multiply. If you note any unusual skin conditions, contact your veterinarian for advice.

Bathing

A Sheltie's skin is much different from a human's. While our skin is dominated by sweat glands, a Sheltie's is very rich in oil glands. These oil glands serve two purposes. First, they help to keep the dog's skin soft and prevent it from becoming dry and cracked. Second, they help to make the dog's coat water-resistant.

With this in mind, it is important that you bathe your Sheltie only when it is absolutely necessary. If the dog's underside or legs are dirty, wash them with a wet towel. If you bathe the dog too often, you will remove the oils from the skin and the dog's coat will become dry. This in turn will cause the

To remove greasy or oily dirt from your Sheltie's coat, rub with margarine or mayonaise and trim off the matted ends. Never use soap or bleach, which would ruin your sheepdog's weather resistant coat.

dog's skin to crack and cause irritation. As a result, the dog will begin to scratch and bite itself, which can lead to the dog getting eczema or other types of infectious diseases. Therefore, bathe your dog only when it is impossible to clean it any other way.

When a bath is necessary, purchase a high-quality dog shampoo. Be sure not to get any shampoo or water in the dog's eyes or ears. After shampooing, be sure to rinse out the shampoo thoroughly. Soap that is not rinsed out may irritate your dog's skin. If you wish, use a cream rinse to give the coat more body and make the hair easier to comb. Then towel the dog dry. Rub the dog briskly with a large towel in order to remove most of the water. Then brush and comb its coat. Keep the dog indoors and away from drafts while it is drying.

When trimming your Sheltie's nails, be sure to clip them at an angle and do not cut the pink area called the quick.

Nail and Tooth, Ear and Eye Care

If your dog is active and gets plenty of exercise, you will not need to trim its nails regularly. However, nails can grow back quickly on a "house dog" and may require frequent trimming. Proper nail care is very important, and I encourage all dog owners to learn how to do it themselves. From the time you first get your puppy you should handle its paws and toes as part of your playing and petting routines. This will alleviate future stress and make nail clipping a quick and painless procedure, rather than a frustrating, exhausting, and futile effort.

Before you trim your dog's nails, be sure you learn how to use a pair of clippers. Improper use of nail clippers can cause your dog a great deal of pain. An experienced dog groomer or a veterinarian can show you how to use clippers. The center of a dog's nail (called the quick) contains a blood vessel and nerve endings. You can see these when you examine the dog's claws. If you cut the quick, your dog will suffer much pain.

The quick grows out as your dog's nail lengthens. If you wait too long between pedicures, you may have to cut the quick in order to clip the nail back to a comfortable length. Always clip the nail

as close to the quick as possible. If you accidentally cut the nail too short, it will bleed. Stop the bleeding by using styptic powder.

Proper tooth care means feeding your dog plenty of hard foods, such as dog biscuits and suitable meat bones or rawhide bones. These foods help prevent the buildup of tartar, which, if left untreated, can cause deterioration of the gums and loss of teeth. In addition, a little lemon juice or fresh tomatoes in your dog's food will help prevent the formation of tartar. Clean your dog's teeth weekly by brushing them with a toothbrush soaked in lemon juice. Thick tartar buildup can be scraped off by your veterinarian.

Ear and eye care is very important; however, I recommend that you first consult a veterinarian for the proper way to clean and care for them. An inexperienced owner can harm a dog seriously by probing around its ears and eyes. The veterinarian can show you how to clean dirt and wax out of the ear and how to clean any sticky discharge that often collects in the corner of a dog's eye. Once you have learned these procedures, you will be able to care for these sensitive organs with confidence.

Caring for a Shetland Sheepdog

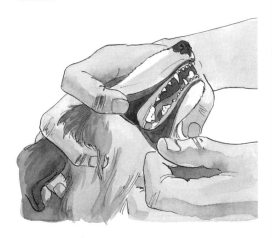

You should regularly check your Sheltie's teeth for tartar build-up.

Lifting and Carrying a Shetland Sheepdog

It is very important for everyone in your family to learn how to lift and carry your puppy. Improper handling can pain and possibly injure the dog. Place one hand under the puppy's chest and support the rear and hind legs with the other hand. Never pick up the puppy by placing only one hand under its abdomen, and never pick it up by the scruff of the neck. Both of these methods can hurt the puppy.

A healthy, adult Sheltie will weigh only fourteen to sixteen pounds, so it can be lifted by most people in the same fashion as a puppy. I do urge you to pick up and carry an adult dog only when necessary. If your Sheltie can jump over an obstacle or climb up a flight of stairs to its destination, then let it. A herding dog needs a lot of exercise.

When moving an injured dog, take special precautions. If possible, wait for an experienced person to lift and carry the dog. If you must do this yourself, first place a muzzle on the dog, for a dog in pain may act unpredictably and snap at anyone who tries to help it. Then place one arm between

the dog's forepaws. The hand on this arm should support the dog's midsection while the dog's head is supported by the forearm. Use the other hand to support the dog's rear and hind legs. Do not allow the dog's midsection to sag or its head to fall forward. For further information on treating an injured dog, consult the chapter, "Ailments and Illnesses" (page 34).

Shetland Sheepdogs and Children

The Shetland sheepdog is a herding breed and when it is with children many of its inbred personality traits become even more evident. Shelties are loyal dogs and are full of pep and spirit. They will joyfully play with children, while at the same time, be alert for any signs of danger. This breed is rarely the aggressor in any confrontation; however, if any

When lifting your puppy, place one hand under the puppy's hindquarters while supporting the abdomen and chest with the other.

Caring for a Shetland Sheepdog

member of its "family" were attacked, the Sheltie would defend that person with a ferocity that belies its small size. Shelties are small, but they are quick to think and maneuver. In addition, their self–assurance and ruggedness make them formidable opponents, even to very large dogs.

A special bond will form between a Sheltie and the children in its "family." Many years of hard life on the Shetland Islands have impressed upon this breed the need to cling to one family, be loyal, and obey their commands.

Although the Sheltie is a hardy and rugged breed, their small bodies will not stand up to all the abuse that many children can dish out. Even the most loyal of Shelties may turn and nip at a child (or adult) it feels is deliberately trying to hurt it. All animals, including humans, have this instinctive defensive reaction. Children should be taught not to pinch and pull on the dog's hair, tail or ears, and always to avoid going near the dog's eyes. Children should be taught never to disturb a Sheltie while it is eating or sleeping. Explain that although the dog is a loving pet, it may nip at them if surprised or frightened. Also teach your children how to meet a strange dog. They should not go to the dog, but let it approach them. They should not move suddenly, and they should keep their hands below the

Children and Shelties can form a life-long bond.

dog's head. If the dog sniffs their hands, and is still friendly, it is all right to pet it.

You can help assure an enduring relationship between your children and your Sheltie by involving them in the responsibilities of dog care. Encourage your children to help feed, groom, and walk your dog.

The Sheltie and the New Baby

Reports of attacks on infants by family dogs lead many people to get rid of their devoted pets when they have a new baby. This is truly a shame, for Shelties are at their best when they have children—including infants—to love. If you have or are planning to have a baby, take heart. Animal behavior experts who have studied this problem thoroughly have concluded that most dogs will not be aggressive toward a baby. They also believe, however, that dogs that tend to chase and kill small animals, or those that are aggressive toward people in general, should never be left unsupervised with an infant.

You should take several precautions to assure your Sheltie's acceptance of your new baby. Before the baby's birth, train your dog to sit or lie down for long periods of time. As you increase the length of time the dog remains still, accustom it to other activities occurring around it at the same time. Reward your dog if it stays still and does not attempt to follow you.

Once training is complete, simulate the other activities that will occur after the baby arrives. Use a doll to imitate carrying, feeding, changing, and bathing the newborn.

After the birth of the infant, give the dog something the baby used in the hospital in order for it to sniff, smell, and become accustomed to the baby's scent. Upon returning home from the hospital, allow the mother to greet the dog without the baby. Then place the baby in the nursery and deny the dog access by using a screen door or folding gate.

Caring for a Shetland Sheepdog

In this way the dog can see and hear the infant and get used to its presence before dog and baby actually meet.

When you finally introduce the dog and baby, one person should control and reward the dog while another person holds the baby. Have the dog sit and then show it to the baby. Keep them together for as long as the dog remains calm. For the next week or two, gradually increase the length of the dog's visit.

Never allow your dog to wander unsupervised in the presence of an infant. However, be sure to allow your dog to be present during activities that involve your newborn. Do not let the dog feel neglected because of the infant. The more activities in which you allow the dog to participate, the stronger the bond will be between Sheltie and child.

Shelties and Other Pets

Shetland sheepdogs should get along well with other pets. Your Sheltie will rarely show signs of jealousy as long as it receives sufficient attention. If there is a substantial size difference, such as with birds, hamsters, gerbils, and so on, it is best not to allow these animals to play freely with your Sheltie.

If you own two Shelties, you will rarely have any problems; in fact, the dogs will probably enjoy each other's companionship. Many individuals of the herding breeds work in tandem with other dogs, and the Sheltie is no exception. You must remember, however, not to give the older dog any less attention than previously. Show the older dog that you care for it as much as always, then leave the two to establish their own relationship. You should have little difficulty getting the two dogs to live in harmony. In fact, if you show no favoritism to either dog, the older one should adopt and protect the younger one.

Before buying a second dog, however, remember that you will need additional equipment, including separate sleeping boxes or cages and food dishes. Also be sure you have the extra time, space, and money that a second dog requires.

The Social Behavior of Dogs

If you plan to own more than one Sheltie, or if you wish to understand why dogs react as they do to humans and to each other, you must examine the dog's instinctive nature.

Canine social behavior is similar to that of wild wolves. Wolves are pack hunting animals and require companionship. This is also true for Shelties, though humans can thoroughly satisfy their need for company. Because of this need, you can punish a dog by isolating it during training sessions. In addition, as pack animals, dogs develop among themselves a dominant–subordinate relationship. This relationship allows a stable existence between dogs. Thus, if one of your dogs tends to be more dominant than another, do not worry. This occurs naturally and will prevent fights between dogs in competition relating to food, living space, and human attention. This social ranking is largely determined by size, age, strength, and sex. This social dominance also allows a dog to obey its owner, for during training a dog learns that it is subordinate to the human members of the household.

Both dogs and wolves "mark" their frequently traveled paths or territory by urinating, defecating, and scratching the ground. In addition to such boundary marking, females secrete a scent that signals their being in heat.

Social Considerations for a Female Dog

If you own a female Shetland sheepdog, you must take special precautions regarding pregnancy. A Sheltie female normally comes into estrus ("in heat" or "in season") twice a year. Estrus is the

Caring for a Shetland Sheepdog

period during which the female accepts mating with the male. This period usually lasts four to fourteen days. If you choose to breed your female, refer to the chapter on breeding (page 48). If you choose not to breed your female, you can take several measures to prevent pregnancy. As stated earlier, if you plan never to breed the female, have her spayed, for the benefits are numerous.

Spaying your female dog will prevent it from roaming away from your home when she is "in season." Also, it is the only sure way to prevent an unwanted litter. Finally, there are many ailments that an unspayed female may suffer that a spayed dog can avoid. These include false pregnancies, uterus infections, ovary cysts, and many types of tumors that attack the reproductive system.

Because spaying a dog is permanent, you must be positive that you will never want to breed your female. If you are at all in doubt, do not have your dog spayed. As your female gets older, you may wish to continue the line of the dog you have grown to love over the years, and you can attempt to do this by breeding your female with another purebred male Sheltie. You cannot do this with a spayed dog. If you decide not to spay, there are other ways to avoid pregnancy in your female dog.

The most obvious way is to keep your female away from all male dogs. This may not be as easy as it sounds. You would be amazed at the distances a male dog will travel to find a female in heat. In addition, stray male dogs may camp outside your house, waiting for you to drop your guard. For this reason you must never let your female go outside alone during estrus. Even if you have a fenced-in yard, she would not be safe. To get at a female in heat, male dogs can perform supercanine feats.

During her "season" your female will also undergo some attitude changes. The mating urge is very great at this time, and your female may be less obedient to your commands, especially if there is a male nearby. So always walk your female on a leash when she is in heat, or you may end up running after her as she ignores your pleas for her to return.

You can consult your veterinarian about additional precautions. Many show dog owners have their veterinarian administer estrus control medication. In this way they can show their females without the worry of "upsetting" the male competition. This drug, however, may have side effects. Chlorophyll tablets are also available through your veterinarian. These tablets help neutralize the odor of the female's secretions.

It is perfectly natural for a female to discharge small amounts of blood during her "season." To prevent staining your rugs or furniture, you may wish to confine her to an easy-to-clean room. Sanitary napkins and diapers are also available for dogs in heat.

Boarding Your Sheltie

During the course of your lives together, it is almost inevitable that you and your Sheltie will have to spend a prolonged period away from each other. You may be suddenly called away from home, or have to go on a business trip, or maybe you need a vacation. If you live alone, or if the other members of your family are going to join you, you must arrange to have someone look after your dog.

Ideal is a dependable neighbor whom the dog knows and trusts and whom you can instruct about your Sheltie's eating, playing, and walking routine. In this way your dog will be able to stay in its familiar environment, your home. Unfortunately things do not always work out this easily.

If you must board your Sheltie, start by contacting the breeder from whom you purchased it. If the breeder is willing to care for your dog, you can be assured of expert care for a Shetland sheepdog. If this is not possible, you may decide to place the dog in a boarding kennel.

Before you leave your Sheltie at a boarding kennel, I recommend that you inspect the facilities thoroughly. Make sure that the sleeping areas and runs are clean and that the operating staff at the

Caring for a Shetland Sheepdog

kennel are knowledgeable. If all the conditions at the boarding facility are suitable to you, there need be little worry about your dog. A mature Shetland sheepdog will have little problem adjusting to this new environment. If it can be avoided, however, you should never leave a puppy younger than six months old, either alone or at a boarding kennel, for a long period of time.

Vacationing with Your Sheltie

Vacationing with your Sheltie can be fun for both of you, but it takes planning. If you plan to travel by air, you will be happy to know that all major airlines will make arrangements to transport your dog. The airline can supply a travel crate and have pressurized cabins where they can house your dog during flight. Before the flight, take your dog for a long walk and allow it to eliminate. It is also good to feed your dog several hours before flying. This will minimize travel sickness. The cost and rules of pet transport service vary from airline to airline, so be sure to check the details ahead of time.

If you decide to vacation in a foreign country, it is advisable to obtain a copy of the country's laws pertaining to dogs from the appropriate consulate. While most countries have minimal regulations about dogs, some do require quarantine. Some countries have laws on the use of muzzles. Most countries do require that your dog be immunized against the major infectious diseases, and you will need a valid health certificate from a licensed veterinarian. If you should require veterinary service while you are abroad, you can get helpful information from the American consulate or embassy.

If you decide to vacation in the United States, you may choose to travel by railroad. Like the airlines, all major railroads will transport dogs. Dogs are usually kept in shipping crates in the baggage car. You can check with the railroad company to see if they will supply the crate.

Traveling by car can be the most fun for your dog. Many Shelties seem to actually enjoy car travel, and will spend hours watching the passing scenery. When traveling by automobile, do not allow your pet to have free run of the car. You should confine your Sheltie to either its cage or the back seat. Open the window enough to give it some fresh air, but do not expose it to a draft. Drafts can cause eye, ear, and throat problems. Make rest stops at least every two hours and allow the dog to walk and relieve itself. Keep it on a leash so that it will not run away. The inside of a car can get very hot, so allow your dog to drink regularly.

Many young dogs may get carsick if they are not used to traveling. As a precaution you can obtain motion sickness tablets from your veterinarian.

Once all your traveling arrangements have been made, it is time to pack. Your sheepdog suitcase should contain the following: food and water dishes, collar, leash, brush, blanket (and cage), and muzzle. It is advisable to bring enough canned or dry food to last the entire trip. If you normally feed your Sheltie fresh foods, accustom it to canned or dry food for a few weeks before your departure.

Safety harnesses, which attach to your car's seat belt clips, can be an invaluable aid when traveling with your Sheltie.

Nutrition

Understanding Nutrition

The nutritional requirements of dogs have probably changed little since they were first trained to perform domestic work. What has changed, however, is our understanding of animal nutrition and our ability to utilize our knowledge to provide our pets with more healthy foods.

All foods are composed of one or several nutrient groups—proteins, fats, carbohydrates, vitamins, minerals, trace elements, and water. These nutrients are essential for the proper growth and metabolism of a dog. By supplying these nutrients in the correct proportions, you will create a well–balanced diet and insure your dog's proper nutrition.

The type and quantity of nutrients a dog needs depends on several factors. Individual growth rate, the kind of work the dog does, exercise, metabolism rate, and many environmental factors all influence the quantity of food your dog requires. For instance, a Shetland sheepdog that spends its days in the hot fields herding sheep requires a higher energy diet than does a Sheltie that spends most of its day confined to a house.

Age is another factor that influences your Sheltie's nutritional requirements. The amount of food a dog needs changes as it gets older. As a result, a dog may become overweight or underweight if its body requirements have changed but its diet has not. For this reason, you must watch your dog's weight and increase or decrease its food intake when necessary.

The Basic Nutrient Groups

Protein

Protein is one of the most important nutrient groups in your dog's diet. Protein supplies amino acids, which are essential for a healthy dog. Recent studies indicate that there are at least ten different types of amino acids required for optimum growth and nitrogen balance in dogs. These are: arginine, histidine, isoleucine, leucine, lysine, methionine, phenylalanine, threonine, tryptophan, and valine. Since a lack of any one of these essential amino acids can result in growth problems, it is best to feed your dog foods that contain a high quantity and variety of dietary proteins. Meat, eggs, fish, milk, and cheese are all excellent sources of protein. In addition, you may add other sources of protein such as wheat germ, soybean meals, and brewer's dried yeast to your dog's diet. One of the best meat sources of protein is beef, which you may feed your dog either raw or cooked. Cooking does not greatly change the protein value, but reduces the fat content somewhat. On the other hand, cooking does break down the vitamins, lessening their nutritional value. Be sure you always cook pork before feeding it to your dog. Pigs are carriers of trichinosis and Aujeszky's disease. All danger of both of these serious diseases can be eliminated by thorough cooking.

Chicken is a good source of easily digestible protein. Because it takes less energy to digest chicken, it is especially good for weak or recuperating dogs. When preparing chicken to feed your dog, it is vitally important to remove all the bones. Because chicken bones are soft and tend to splinter, a Sheltie can suffer great harm if it chews and swallows them. These splinters can cut and seriously damage a dog's mouth, throat, and digestive tract.

When heeling, your Sheltie(s) should walk at your side with their heads as far forward as your front knee. If they stray ahead, restrain them with the leash while using the proper verbal command and hand signal.

Many of the signs of protein deficiency are non-specific and can be created by other dietary deficiencies as well. A diet deficient in protein may cause poor growth, weight loss, decreased appetite, blood formation problems, edema, and decreased milk production. Protein deficiencies may also result in poor hair and coat condition and a reduction in antibodies, which can make a dog more susceptible to numerous diseases.

Fat

Fat is an important part of an active Sheltie's diet. Fat is a concentrated source of energy, and it also provides essential fatty acids. Fatty acids are necessary for metabolic regulation and serve structural functions in cell membranes. The essential fatty acids and the fat-soluble vitamins (A, D, and E) are necessary for the proper development of a Sheltie's skin and coat.

Because fats are such an essential part of a Sheltie's diet, it is important to restrict the fat content only if your dog becomes obese. An active Sheltie that is put on a low-fat diet may quickly show signs of problems. Fat deficiency, which is very rare, could result in the hair becoming coarse and dry and the appearance of skin lesions. Most meats and meat products contain an amount of fat sufficient to meet an active Sheltie's needs.

Carbohydrates

Carbohydrates include starches and sugars. All dogs require certain sugars in order to provide en-

Shelties are alert, loyal, and obedient dogs. They respond with serious attention in obedience class and disciplined enthusiasm when learning to jump hurdles.

ergy for internal organs and the central nervous system. Thus, carbohydrates help regulate your Sheltie's energy balance. If a Sheltie's diet lacks carbohydrates, its body will convert proteins normally used for growth into needed sugars. This in turn can cause protein deficiencies.

Complex carbohydrates also supply fibers and roughage, which provide bulk needed to promote regularity and prevent intestinal problems such as diarrhea or constipation. Most commercial diets provide an ample amount of necessary carbohydrates. If you are preparing your Sheltie's food from scratch, you should add some complex carbohydrates to its diet. Sources include rice, corn, potatoes, oats, wheat, and cereals. Boiling, toasting, or baking will make it easier for your dog to digest these foods.

Vitamins

The importance of vitamins in preventing illness and in regulating many canine body functions has been well documented. Deficiencies of the essential vitamins have been known to cause skin lesions, conjunctivitis, osteoporosis, muscle weakness, depression, rickets, and nervous disorders, to name only a few ailments. Vitamins are also extremely important in assuring proper growth and fertility.

It is best to consult your veterinarian when choosing a vitamin supplement for your Sheltie's diet. Studies have shown that an excess of some vitamins may be just as harmful to your pet as a lack of them. In preparing your dog's diet you may choose to add fresh greens, carrots, and fruits, for these are good sources of many vitamins. Other vitamin-enriched foods include brewer's yeast, cod-liver oil, and wheat germ oil.

It is important to remember that cooking your Sheltie's food can greatly reduce the vitamin content of the diet. Many vitamins are unstable, and can be destroyed by heat or rancidity. So be sure to serve only fresh, uncooked foods as vitamin supplements.

Nutrition

Minerals

Minerals, like vitamins, are needed for the proper performance of many canine body functions. In addition, minerals are vital in maintaining the acid–base balance in your Sheltie's body.

The two minerals that dogs need the most are calcium and phosphorus. When supplied in the right proportions, calcium and phosphorus, along with Vitamin D, are used to develop strong bones and teeth in puppies and young dogs. In recent years there has been much talk about how increased calcium levels can prevent osteoporosis, a condition in adult dogs that is caused by a loss of bone and the subsequent fractures that soon follow. Recent reports, however, indicate that there is not necessarily a relationship between calcium intake and osteoporosis. In fact, these studies indicate that an excessive amount of calcium can lead to the development of skeletal deformities. If you choose to prepare your Sheltie's food fresh, you can provide your dog with sufficient calcium and phosphorus by giving it soft ribs and calf bones to chew on. Calcium phosphate tablets are also available. However, because of the dangers of excess calcium, your veterinarian should establish the dosage.

Salt is another mineral source, and it is necessary to maintain a proper water balance. Shelties not supplied with an adequate amount of salt tend to fatigue easily and may suffer from dry skin and a loss of hair. Because most commercial foods contain an adequate amount of salt, there is usually little need for salt supplementation. By the same token, never intentionally reduce your dog's salt intake unless you have consulted a veterinarian.

Trace Elements

Trace elements (including cobalt, copper, iodine, iron, manganese, selenium, and zinc) are so named because they are needed only in small quantities. Enough of these elements is found in an otherwise adequate diet to meet the needs of a Shetland sheepdog.

Water

Water is an extremely important component of the diet, because it is vital to all living cells. The body of an adult Sheltie contains nearly 60% water. Because a dog's body cannot store much water, an inadequate supply can quickly cause problems and even death. A dog's water intake depends on such factors as air temperature, type of food, amount of exercise, and temperament. Your dog should have water available at all times, or at least three times a day. Never give your dog a great deal of cold water after strenuous exercise, for this can make it ill.

You can purchase commercial dog food that can supply your Shetland sheepdog with virtually every essential nutrient. If you wish to prepare your dog's food yourself, however, by all means do so. Just bear in mind that this may be significantly more expensive and quite time–consuming.

As stated earlier, the quantity of food your dog requires depends on numerous individual and environmental factors. Ask your veterinarian for rec-

Proper nourishment is essential for your Sheltie's health.

ommendations regarding a well–balanced, fortified diet.

Feeding from Scratch

If you choose to prepare your Sheltie's food yourself, you can follow the following recommended proportions. Choose and combine foods from each nutritional group so that for young dogs you have 70% protein foods and 30% carbohydrates. The 70% protein foods should supply 5–10% fat. For adult dogs choose 50% proteins, 50% carbohydrates, with proteins supplying 5–10% fat. For both young and old Shelties, supplement the food with vitamins and minerals as recommended by your veterinarian.

Commercial Dog Foods

Commercial dog foods offer many advantages over preparing your dog's meal from scratch. The most obvious advantage is ease of preparation. Perhaps the most important advantage is that they can supply almost 100% of the nutritional value your dog needs.

Be aware that not all commercial dog foods are the same. Basically there are three different types of commercial dog food available: dry, semimoist, and moist. In addition to the differences among these three types of food, there are also differences from brand to brand. So be sure to read the labels carefully for nutritional information and feeding tips.

Dry dog foods come in pellets, kibbles, extruded products, or whole biscuits. These foods, as the name suggests, are low in moisture (10–12%). They contain mostly grains, cereal by–products, soybean and animal meals, milk products, and fats, as well as vitamin and mineral supplements.

Semimoist dog foods usually contain 25–30%

moisture. Generally preservatives have been added to protect against spoilage without refrigeration. These foods contain many of the same ingredients as the dry type, but usually have less meat meals and more whole meat. Semimoist foods are usually shaped into patties or simulated meat chunks.

Canned dog foods are usually very high in moisture (about 75%). Be sure to check the information on the labels. Some types are nutritionally complete and can be served alone; other kinds are a highly palatable food supplement that can be added to nutritionally complete dry foods to make them more appealing.

Choosing the type of commercial dog food may become confusing because there are many successful formulas, and many of them may differ greatly in their ingredients. Thankfully, Shelties, like most other dogs, are very adaptable, and they will eat almost any commercial dog food that is offered to them. It is best, however, not to keep changing your Sheltie's food. Changes in your dog's diet can cause numerous digestive side effects, such as diarrhea or constipation. Once you have found an adequate and successful diet, keep your Sheltie on it.

If you give your dog a well–balanced diet, it will thrive on it for its entire life. Although I am not implying that giving your dog a variety of foods is bad, a dog will not become tired of the "same old thing" if it is not given a variety of foods. If your dog does not eat, something is wrong emotionally or physically. It may be no more than a mild stomach upset; however, if your dog falls off its diet for three or four days, take it to your veterinarian.

Feeding by Age

Puppies under Five Months Old

For the first eight weeks of its life, all the nourishment a puppy needs is supplied by its mother. Once the puppy is weaned, it is your responsibility to feed it properly. A puppy's body is constantly

Nutrition

undergoing changes associated with normal growth and development. A puppy, therefore, requires about twice the amount of nutrients per pound of body weight as a fully grown adult dog.

Because a puppy grows extremely rapidly, it is important that it get substantial protein. Purchase a high–quality commercial puppy food and add eggs, diced beef or chicken, milk, or cottage cheese to it. A Sheltie puppy may eat the equivalent of 10% of its body weight daily. Feed a puppy younger than five months old three times a day.

Start feeding your puppy the same food, and on the same schedule used by the breeder. Sudden changes in a puppy's diet can cause digestive disorders. If you do decide that you want to change your puppy's diet, do it gradually. Start by adding a small amount of the new food to the puppy's accustomed food. Slowly increase the proportion of new food, so that it will take a few weeks to totally change over to the new diet.

Always serve your puppy's food at room temperature, and always keep a fresh supply of water in your puppy's dish. Make sure the water is not too cold, especially during the winter, for this can give the puppy chills. Also, be sure to thoroughly wash your puppy's food dish and water dish every day. Harmful bacteria can grow quickly in bowls that are not regularly cleaned. Bacteria can be extremely dangerous to young puppies, whose immune system may still be weak.

At 14 weeks of age, the puppy's permanent teeth will begin to push through the gums, causing pain. To ease the puppy's discomfort, let it chew on a rawhide bone, or a hard beef bone of manageable size. If you should decide not to use a bone, then be prepared. Your puppy may decide to ease the pain by gnawing on the leg of a chair, table, or perhaps that new pair of leather shoes!

Puppies Five to Seven Months Old

Puppies at this age do not need to be fed as often, so reduce the feeding to two times a day. Watch your puppy's weight carefully. If your dog becomes too fat or too thin, increase or decrease its food intake accordingly. During this period you will probably continue to increase your puppy's food because it is still growing. Add vitamin and mineral supplements as advised to do so by your veterinarian.

Puppies Seven to Ten Months Old

At this age your dog is about to reach maturity, and its growth rate will be decreasing. Your Sheltie will therefore require less food. Though it is best to continue to feed your dog two meals a day, begin to serve smaller portions. At this point you should purchase a commercial diet suitable for older puppies. If you wish, you can supplement with meat, chicken, and other suitable table scraps.

Note: Never feed salty or spicy table scraps to any dog. One piece of salty ham, for example, can seriously harm your pet's kidneys.

Adult Dogs

Coat condition and physical activity are the best indicators of a properly fed dog. A proper diet produces a smooth, soft, shiny coat with rich color. Improperly fed dogs have dull, coarse coats and appear lethargic and fatigued.

How much you feed your adult Sheltie depends on its weight and activity. An outgoing sheepdog used for herding needs a higher energy food and more of it than a Sheltie that gets less exercise. In addition, temperament, age, and sex all have a bearing on how much food the dog requires. The best way to monitor how much food your dog needs is to weigh it every few weeks. If your dog is gaining weight, reduce its food and fat intake and give it more exercise.

Environment also has a large bearing on a Sheltie's food intake. A dog kept in an outdoor run in cold weather needs more than 50% more calories than it would if kept in a warm environment.

Although an adult dog is no longer growing, its digestive system needs to be in steady working condition so the dog may maintain a healthy metabolism and absorb nutrients properly. To satisfy this need, decrease the protein in your adult dog's diet and increase the complex carbohydrates. Complex carbohydrates, which are high in fiber and roughage, increase bulk and promote healthy digestion.

Older Dogs

Over the past two decades there has been a steady increase in the "geriatric" portion of the canine population in the United States. This increase is mainly due to advances in preventing infectious diseases and a better understanding of canine nutrition. Recent studies conclude that older dogs, like growing puppies, require a diet higher in protein and lower in fat.

It is believed that as a dog becomes older it be-

gins to lose its ability to utilize fat. So instead of using fat for energy, it begins to store it, and thereby becomes overweight. At the same time, the older dog would require more protein in its diet to make up for the inability to burn up fat. There are ongoing studies to determine the exact nutritional requirements of the older dog. However, at present, many experts agree that older dogs should be fed a diet of greater than 15% protein.

There are several commercial dog foods that cater to the adult dog. If you wish, you can supplement this diet with high-quality protein sources such as eggs, liver, milk, or cottage cheese. Be careful with the amount of these calorie-dense supplements. Older dogs can quickly become overweight if fed a calorie-rich diet. Just remember to be sensible and cut back on your dog's diet if it begins to become overweight.

Ailments and Illnesses

Understanding Symptoms of Disease

Abnormal symptoms indicate that your dog is not well and that medical treatment may be necessary. A single abnormal symptom, or a combination of them, does not always point to a specific illness. It usually takes the training of a veterinarian to discover the cause of the problem.

Watch for loss of or excessive appetite or thirst, physical exhaustion, poor coat condition, excessive coughing or sneezing, frequent wheezing or running nose, repeated vomiting, pale gums, foul breath, slight paralysis or limping, trembling or shaking, sudden weight loss, any swelling or lumps on the body, cloudy or orange–colored urine, inability to urinate or uncontrollable urge to urinate, diarrhea, moaning or whimpering, a discharge from the eyes, and any unusual slobbering or salivation. If you notice any one or a combination of these symptoms, contact your veterinarian. Many diseases can cause severe damage if not treated promptly.

Two of the most common abnormal symptoms are vomiting and diarrhea. They occur frequently in dogs and do not always indicate a serious ailment. Therefore, they warrant further discussion.

Vomiting

Vomiting does not always indicate a problem. A mother with newborn puppies may instinctively regurgitate food in an attempt to feed her pups. In addition, young dogs, especially puppies, often attack their food so greedily that their natural defense mechanisms send the food back up again. This behavior disappears as they mature. Nervous dogs may also vomit whenever something bothers them.

Vomiting is considered significant only when it occurs persistently. Vomiting can be caused by internal parasites, an infection, numerous digestive ailments, and other diseases. Persistent vomiting is usually accompanied by irregular bowel movements such as diarrhea. A dog with these symptoms needs veterinary attention.

Diarrhea

An occasional soft stool need not worry you, although diarrhea may follow. Continued watery bowel movements, however, indicate a serious ailment. Diarrhea, like vomiting, is a symptom of nearly every canine ailment, including distemper, worms, poisoning, nervous disorders, parvovirus, and intestinal blockages.

If diarrhea occurs infrequently and your dog seems otherwise healthy, it may indicate a minor stomach or intestinal upset, or perhaps an emotional upset. You can help an occasional attack of diarrhea by regulating your dog's diet. Do not give liquids such as milk or broth in food. Provide plenty of water and thoroughly cooked starches such as rice or oatmeal. If it does not clear up after a few days, take your dog to your veterinarian. If left untreated, diarrhea can lead to dehydration and death. If you see any blood in your dog's stool, contact your veterinarian immediately.

Preventive Medicine

You can take many preventive measures to keep your dog from becoming ill. Prevention starts with a well–balanced diet. Proper hygiene, an adequate exercise program, and a satisfactory dog–owner relationship are also important. Finally, be sure to have your puppy vaccinated against infectious diseases.

Vaccinations

Dogs are vaccinated to prevent them from contracting infectious diseases. These diseases are usually caused by bacteria or viruses and can spread rapidly throughout the dog population. Vaccinations do not always guarantee permanent protection, and often annual booster shots are necessary.

Reputable breeders vaccinate their puppies before selling them, and should supply you with a record of all medical treatments. It takes three or

Ailments and Illnesses

four weeks for an immunization to become fully effective. You should keep a record of all of your dog's immunizations. (You will need this record if you plan to travel abroad with your dog). These records remind you of the need for booster shots.

Canine Distemper was once second only to rabies as the most dangerous known dog disease. A highly contagious virus, it is spread through the urine, feces, saliva, and even nasal discharge of the infected animal. The virus may also be carried on blankets, brushes, and clothing. Now, however, dogs vaccinated against distemper will not contract the disease easily.

If the puppy's mother was properly vaccinated against distemper, she is able to passively immunize her newborn puppies. Such immunization lasts through nursing. After weaning, the puppies will need additional vaccinations. Bear in mind that canine distemper is dangerous and can be very difficult to treat. Thus, vaccinating your dog is extremely important.

Early symptoms of distemper include high fever, diarrhea, dry cough, depression, and watery discharge from the eyes and nose. Advanced symptoms may include cramps, loss of equilibrium, twitching of leg and facial muscles, partial paralysis, and convulsive seizures. Vaccinations and booster shots are the only effective protection against this disease. Canine distemper is almost always fatal to a young dog that has not been immunized. In older dogs, the disease may cause damage of the central nervous system.

Canine Hepatitis should not be confused with human hepatitis. Canine hepatitis is caused by a virus that primarily attacks the liver and gastrointestinal tract. Dogs contract this virus in much the same manner as they do canine distemper. Although humans may carry the virus on their clothing, they cannot catch it. Vaccinated dogs rarely contract this disease. Canine hepatitis is almost always fatal to an unvaccinated puppy, however. Veterinarians can sometimes save an adult dog.

The symptoms of canine hepatitis include high fever, diarrhea, inflammation of the nasal passages, severe thirst, listlessness, and liver inflammation that makes the abdomen sensitive to the touch. A dog with canine hepatitis also tends to arch its back and rub its belly on the floor in an attempt to relieve the pain in its liver and stomach. Canine hepatitis develops very rapidly; a dog may appear healthy one day and very ill the next.

Leptospirosis is caused by bacteria transmitted through the urine of rats, mice, or an infected dog. Dogs must ingest the bacteria to contract the disease, which attacks the kidneys and liver.

The symptoms of leptospirosis are very similar to those of canine distemper and canine hepatitis; however, leptospirosis usually causes a kidney infection that changes the color and odor of the urine. The urine of an infected dog has a deep yellow to orange color and a strong, offensive odor.

Leptospirosis causes a dog great pain; if not treated in its early stages, it is almost always fatal. On very rare occasions, leptospirosis has been transmitted to humans. Vaccinations against this disease are the only way to protect your dog, yourself, and your family.

Parainfluenza refers to various viruses that can infect the upper respiratory system. Also known as kennel cough, it causes inflammation of the trachea and the bronchi, and is common whenever and wherever dogs congregate. If you plan to board your dog in a kennel or an animal hospital, you should see that it is vaccinated against these diseases.

Rabies is a viral infection that attacks the nervous system of all warm–blooded animals, including humans. It is usually transmitted through a bite in which the infected saliva of a rabid animal enters the victim's body. The virus can also be contracted if the saliva makes contact with an open wound.

Early symptoms of rabies include behavioral changes. An infected dog may be irritable one minute and friendly the next. Later symptoms include frequent urination and attempts to bite or eat foreign objects such as wood and stones. The dog then becomes vicious, drools excessively, and has difficulty swallowing. Finally, the dog becomes par-

Ailments and Illnesses

alyzed, cannot eat or drink, and dies shortly thereafter.

Every dog should be vaccinated against rabies. Because rabies is dangerous to humans as well as dogs, the disease is considered a public health hazard. Any suspicion of rabies should be reported to public health authorities.

Parvovirus began to appear in dogs only a few years ago. Puppies should be vaccinated before their 14th week. The virus is carried and transmitted in much the same way as canine distemper.

Two forms of parvovirus are known. One causes an inflammation of the heart muscles of very young puppies. Infected animals quickly collapse and die of heart failure. The more common form, parvoviral enteritis, is characterized by constant vomiting of a foamy, yellow–brown liquid and bloody, foul–smelling diarrhea. Patting the abdomen of an infected dog will cause it to wince in pain. Parvoviral enteritis occurs in dogs of all ages and results in heavy loss of fluids. This leads to severe dehydration and death within a few days.

If the disease is detected early enough, an unvaccinated dog can be saved by intense treatment with infusions and antibiotics. However, immunization against parvovirus is the best way to protect your dog.

Note: The vaccination against parvovirus must frequently be repeated to be fully effective. Yearly boosters are recommended.

Vaccination Schedule

Prior to Mating: If you intend to breed your female, bring her to your veterinarian prior to her "season." She can then receive any necessary booster shots and have her stool checked for worms. This will give her puppies passive immunity for about four to six weeks, provided she will nurse them.

Temporary Immunizations: Starting at four to six weeks of age, a puppy's passive immunity (conveyed by milk from the mother) begins to wear off.

Your veterinarian will then administer a series of immunizations that require periodic boosters. Your puppy should receive shots against distemper, canine hepatitis, leptospirosis, parainfluenza, and parvovirus. Then every three or four weeks, until your puppy is four months old, it should receive the necessary booster shots.

Booster Shots: By having your dog vaccinated regularly, you can provide it maximum protection against these infectious diseases. Your veterinarian will explain the frequency for each type of booster, which ranges from six months for parvovirus to three years for rabies.

Internal Parasites

Roundworms are by far the most common internal parasites found in dogs. They are white, cylindrical in shape, and can grow up to 4 inches (10 cm). The adult worm embeds itself in the dog's intestinal tract to lay eggs. The eggs are then passed through the dog's stool. If ingested by another animal the eggs will grow into adult worms inside the host and continue the cycle. Although roundworms rarely cause serious illness in adult dogs, they can be fatal to a heavily infested puppy. Roundworms are frequently found in newborn puppies if their mother was infected during pregnancy.

Symptoms of roundworm infestation include irregular appetite, diarrhea, weakness, cramps, bloated belly, and in severe cases, paralysis. In addition, the dog's anus may itch, in which case it will skid its rump across the floor in an attempt to scratch it.

Tapeworms infiltrate young and adult dogs and are very tenacious. The head of this worm has hooks and suckers that it uses to attach itself to the dog's small intestine. There it grows into a long chain of segments. The tail segment contains many eggs; occasionally the worm releases the segments, which are passed in the dog's stool. (The segments

Ailments and Illnesses

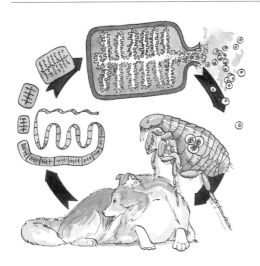

The life cycle of the tapeworm. Egg-filled segments are passed out in the dog's feces where they are picked up by fleas, which may then be injested by a dog. Uncooked meat or fish may also be a source of tapeworm eggs.

a dog, the larvae can enter the dog's bloodstream. It takes about six months for the larvae to develop into mature worms.

You can prevent heartworms by using diethyl-carbomozine (available from your veterinarian). You should use this drug only if your Sheltie has been tested and found free of adult heartworms, because the drug can be extremely harmful to an infested dog. Your dog should be tested annually for heartworms prior to the mosquito season.

Note: Heartworm is a parasite that is prevalent in certain areas. Do not treat your dog with heartworm medication unless you have been informed of heartworm prevalence in your area and unless your dog has been tested. Remember, too, to ask about heartworm when traveling with your pet.

There are also many other forms of worms including hookworms, kidney worms, lung worms, and whipworms. Each type has different symptoms and will often require special medication. For this reason you should contact your veterinarian

look like grains of rice and often adhere to the hairs surrounding the anus.)

Symptoms of tapeworm infestation, which are similar to those of roundworm infections, may take a long time to develop. Tapeworms are usually diagnosed by examining the stool. Fleas are the most common source of tapeworms, although your Sheltie may also get them from eating infected, uncooked meat (especially pork and lamb). Your veterinarian will treat tapeworms with a medication specifically for this disease.

Heartworm infestation is very serious and can be fatal if not treated promptly. Heartworms attach themselves to the right side of the heart and parts of the lungs. They cause the heart to work harder. As a result, the dog's heart ages rapidly and eventually weakens.

Heartworms are transmitted by mosquitoes that carry the worms' larvae. When the mosquito bites

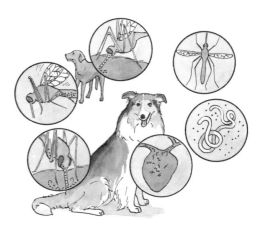

The life cycle of the heartworm. Mosquitoes carry the larvae and pass them into the bloodstream. The larvae seek out and grow in the dog's heart.

Ailments and Illnesses

promptly if you suspect your Sheltie is infested. Owners can do more damage than good to their dogs when they experiment with worming medications.

Many puppies are wormed before leaving the breeder, and you should obtain a written record of worming for your veterinarian. When you bring your puppy to the veterinarian for a checkup or for its booster shots, bring a sample of its stool in a plastic bag. Your veterinarian will examine the stool for evidence of infestation.

External Parasites

Fleas are the most common of all canine parasites. They cause more suffering to dogs than any other ailment. They differ from other parasites in that they jump; and they can jump a great distance from one dog to another. Fleas crawl under a dog's thick coat, biting and sucking blood. This causes severe itching, and by scratching the dog may develop eczema. You may find fleas very difficult to eliminate.

Buy a flea spray or powder in your pet store. Spray or powder the entire dog, as directed on the label. Be sure to cover the dog's eyes and nose with your hand while spraying. Both sprays and powders can irritate the mucous membranes. A flea shampoo is also highly effective and less likely to cause allergic reactions. You must also disinfect all areas where your dog may have caught the fleas, including its kennel or run, its blanket and sleeping box, and your furniture and carpets (if your dog has had any contact with them).

Lice, like all other external parasites, burrow into one area, suck blood, and cause irritation. You can see clusters of eggs on your dog's hairs if it is infested. Lice can be very dangerous, so bring your dog to your veterinarian promptly if you spot them. The doctor can eliminate the lice using an insecticide dip.

Ticks are bloodsuckers that, once embedded, hang on tenaciously. Ticks can carry serious diseases such as Rocky Mountain Spotted Fever. Another infection transmitted through ticks is Lyme disease. In recent years the number of infected dogs has risen dramatically in the northeastern and midwestern portions of the United States. A dog infected with Lyme disease (named after the Connecticut town where the ailment was first noted in humans) exhibits symptoms of stiffness, pain, fever, inflammation of joints, and rashes. If caught early enough, Lyme disease can be cured with antibiotic therapy, with tetracycline being the drug of choice.

Another tick–borne disease that has long affected animals and is now appearing in both dogs and humans is babesiasis. In dogs, babesiasis causes fever, anorexia, lethargy, depression, pallor, and rapid pulse rate.

The increase in reported cases of tick–borne diseases is most likely due to the increasing population of host animals (raccoons, deer, and opossum) moving into areas in which they have been scarce before. The ticks will then leave the animal it has infected and will seek a new host such as a dog or a human.

Humans cannot "catch" a tick–borne disease from a dog; however, they can become infected by the same tick that is transmitting the disease. It is impossible to eradicate ticks from all areas, but try to keep your dog away from known tick–infested areas such as open fields and woods. It is also a good practice to inspect your dog for ticks each time it returns to the house. Be sure to check inside the ears and between the toes, for these are a tick's favorite location.

To remove a tick, first wash the infected area with alcohol, which helps to loosen the tick's grasp. When you have loosened it somewhat, place a pair of tweezers squarely over the tick and carefully lift it off. Be careful not to pull the body apart; you must remove it whole. If the head remains under the dog's skin, it can cause an infection. Once you have removed the tick, place it in the middle of your toilet and flush. However, if you suspect the tick of being a disease-carrier, you should place it in a tightly sealed jar and bring it to your veterinarian for examination.

Never attempt to remove a tick with a lighted match or with your bare fingers, because it is possible to contract these diseases from contact with the tick. If your dog begins to show signs of tick–borne diseases, take your dog to a veterinarian immediately.

Mites, like fleas, cause intense itching. Hence, a dog that scratches and chews at its skin may not be suffering from flea infestation. Symptoms such as red dots, pimples, damp spots, crusty scaly skin, greasy skin, or loss of hair can mean eczema, mites, nutritional deficiencies, hormonal imbalances, allergies, and so on. Consult your veterinarian regarding the diagnosis and treatment of these ailments.

Mange, a serious skin disease, can exhibit these symptoms. Mange is caused by mites, parasites no larger than a pinhead. The two principal forms of mange are sarcoptic mange and demodectic mange. Sarcoptic mange is usually easier to recognize because it makes the dog more miserable and causes more scratching. The affected area becomes red and full of bloody sores and scabs. The skin thickens and feels leathery. The dog's hair sheds completely in the affected area. The disease then begins to spread, and the dog produces an odor similar to that of strong cheese or that associated with a foot problem.

Demodectic mange is harder to detect because sometimes it results only in slight hair loss and some reddening and inflammation of the affected skin. Sometimes bloody pimples form that can burst and become infected. This condition does not always cause a great deal of itching or irritation. The only signs of demodectic mange may be a small lesion about ½ inch (1 cm) in diameter marked by hair loss or a small bald spot.

Your veterinarian can identify either type of mange by taking skin scrapings and examining them under a microscope.

Other Skin Disorders

Additional skin disorders include allergies, eczema, and ringworm. Allergic symptoms may be similar to those of other skin ailments: inflammation, itching, pimples, flaking or scaling, and sometimes skin loss. Treatment usually takes time; first your veterinarian must diagnose the specific cause.

Eczema is a general name for several different skin irritations. Eczema occurs in either wet or dry patches, and it may have many causes, including dietary deficiencies of vitamin A and fat, exposure to dampness or excessive heat, hormone imbalance, and parasites.

Ringworm is not a worm but a fungus. It affects the outer layer of a dog's skin. It may cause inflammation, itching, hair loss, and scabby areas. It may be transmitted from an infected dog to a human, so prompt veterinary treatment is essential.

Note: If ringworm is suspected in a human, it should also be diagnosed and treated at once.

Digestive Disorders

Constipation

Constipation occurs when solid waste products that cannot be easily passed build up in the dog's digestive tract. Generally this can be relieved by changing the dog's diet and by including a mild laxative. Half a cup of lukewarm milk hourly can also be most effective. You should reduce dry bulk foods in your dog's diet until the stool is normal.

Constipation may also be caused by eating an indigestible object, such as a small toy or a stone. If you suspect this, call your veterinarian immediately. Do not give your dog a laxative if you suspect a foreign object. This may require surgery.

Enteritis

Inflammation of the intestine may be caused by bacteria, poisons, worms, ulcers, the swallowing of

Ailments and Illnesses

sharp objects, etc. Regardless of the cause, any inflammation of the intestinal tract is called enteritis. This condition may be accompanied by diarrhea or foul–smelling stools. Enteritis may cause the dog much discomfort, resulting in its lying in unusual and contorted positions when at rest. Almost all intestinal ailments require professional care, so if these symptoms appear, contact your veterinarian immediately.

Throat and Respiratory Ailments

Dogs can contract most common throat and respiratory ailments, including coughs, asthma, bronchitis, laryngitis, and pneumonia. Dogs do not suffer from the common cold, but are subject to a similar respiratory ailment. Symptoms include runny nose, thin mucus discharge from the eyes, slight fever, chills, coughing, and sneezing.

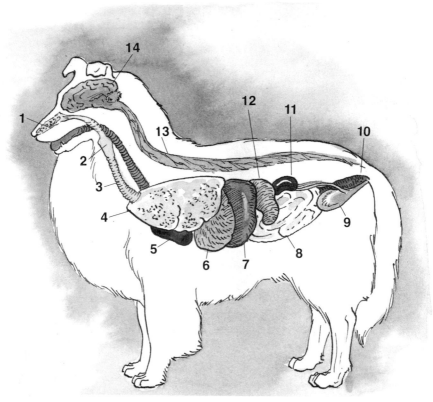

The digestive, respiratory, and nervous systems of the Shetland sheepdog:
1. sinus cavity 2. thyroid cartilage 3. trachea 4. lungs 5. heart 6. liver 7. stomach 8. small intestines 9. bladder 10. rectum 11. kidneys 12. spleen 13. spinal column 14. brain

Ailments and Illnesses

Tonsillitis

Tonsillitis, an inflammation of the tonsils, is usually caused by an infection. A dog with tonsillitis may run a high fever, refuse to eat, drool, and vomit frequently and violently. Your veterinarian can treat tonsillitis with appropriate medication; only rarely is surgery required.

Parainfluenza

Frequently called "kennel cough," parainfluenza is a common respiratory ailment in dogs. It responds to treatment readily, especially in the early stages. Immunization, with annual boosters, has also proven effective (see page 36).

Pneumonia

Once a common killer of dogs pneumonia is now treated successfully with antibiotics. Pneumonia is characterized by a cough, shallow breathing, nasal discharge, loss of appetite, and high fever.

Yearly eye checks can help detect eye ailments in their early stages, which in many cases can make treatment much easier and more effective.

Most respiratory ailments can be treated with antibiotics. Take your dog to your veterinarian if it shows signs of severe respiratory problems.

Eye Disorders

While there are few Shetland sheepdogs that suffer from major eye disorders, collie–eye seems to be the most common. The collie–eye abnormality is an inherited ocular defect that is present from birth. The disease does have associated symptoms that can be detected only by a veterinarian. The eyes of the affected Sheltie may be small or more deeply set.

While visual loss occurs in fewer than one percent of the affected dogs, if the disease causes a detachment of the retina, it will cause blindness. It is wise to check for inherited eye disorders before breeding your Sheltie.

Ear Ailments

Shelties suffer from few ear ailments; however, if you suspect an ear problem, leave the dog's ear alone and contact your veterinarian. An inexperienced owner who probes too far into the sensitive ear canal can cause the dog additional damage.

Symptoms of ear disorders include persistent shaking of the head, rubbing of the ears with paws or on the floor, cocking the head at an unusual angle, and any type of discharge from the ear. The insides of the dog's ears may appear reddish and inflamed.

Collie Nose

While this disease is not believed to be inherited, it is one that is present from birth. Collie nose is an abnormal reaction of the skin to sunlight and

Ailments and Illnesses

The checking of your Sheltie's inner ear should be left to the veterinarian.

is most common in collies, Shetland sheepdogs, and German shepherd dogs. This disease, which is characterized by dermatitis or eczema, primarily affects the dog's nose, eyes, and adjacent areas.

The progress of the disease is slow; at first it may appear to be a light reddening of the muzzle skin. As the disease progresses, the skin on the bridge of the nose becomes markedly irritated and lesions may begin to occur. The dog may contract conjunctivitis, and the skin around the face and eyes becomes pink to bright red and sore. This disease can be controlled but not cured by the application of topical medications. Lesions caused by this disease are more intense in the summer and subside during the winter. This condition can also be greatly improved by keeping your dog away from sunlight.

Other Disorders

Hip Dysplasia

Hip dysplasia is a developmental disease of the hip joints. This ailment occurs most commonly in young dogs of larger breeds; therefore, Shelties are not as susceptible as their larger cousins, the collie. The disease itself is due to a hip socket malformation that does not allow for the proper fit of the head of the femur.

At birth, the hip of a dog with severe hip dysplasia appears normal; signs of the disorder do not appear until the dog is five months or older. The optimum age for a definite diagnosis is between 24 and 36 months. Hip dysplasia results in painful inflammation of the hip joint, which leads to permanent physical damage, including lameness and the loss of the use of the back legs.

It is now possible for veterinarians to surgically correct the shape of the hip socket. Another surgical procedure, known as total hip replacement, has been highly successful. Unfortunately, these procedures are performed only by a limited number of specialists, and they can be quite costly.

It is estimated that only a small percentage of Shetland sheepdogs suffer from this disease, which has low to moderate heritability. However, Shelties with hip dysplasia should *never* be used by breeders.

False Pregnancy

False pregnancies are imagined pregnancies in which the female behaves as if she were pregnant but does not have any fetuses in her uterus.

A female behaves during a false pregnancy as she would during a real one. She creeps off by herself, runs around restlessly, and paws at her bed. She also tends to carry toys, stuffed animals, or an old shoe to her bed, and defends them as if they were puppies. The biggest problem is that she may become overly aggressive in protecting her "offspring."

Usually this condition disappears by itself, and the female returns to normal behavior. If it occurs several times a year, take your dog to your veterinarian. Although hormone therapy relieves the signs of false pregnancy, it is rarely recommended because it may cause further complications.

Ailments and Illnesses

Your veterinarian may suggest the surgical removal of the ovaries. This is safe, will spare your dog a great deal of pain, and may even prolong her life. Removal of the ovaries prevents recurrence of false pregnancy, which can lead to uterine infections. The surgery should not be performed while the symptoms of false pregnancy are still apparent, however, because the protective behavior may persist. Postpone surgery until all symptoms have disappeared.

Shock

Shock is a serious condition that results from a traumatic physical or emotional experience. The most common cause is an automobile accident. A dog in shock may appear asleep, or it may be semiconscious. Symptoms vary according to the severity of the condition. Breathing may be shallow, the dog's body may be cold, and its pulse may be rapid.

If your dog is in shock, try to calm it in a soft voice, pet it reassuringly, and if possible, cover it with a blanket or an article of clothing. Because the actions of a dog in shock are unpredictable, use caution in handling it. Take it to a veterinarian immediately.

Broken bones also frequently result from automobile accidents. A dog with a fracture will be in severe pain. Therefore, always remember to approach an injured dog very carefully, as it may attempt to bite you. If a dog has a compound fracture (one in which the broken bone punctures the skin), cover the wound with gauze or a clean cloth to help prevent infections. Your veterinarian will set the fracture.

Poisoning

Although this section contains general information on poisoning, it is important for you to call directory assistance now and obtain the telephone number of the nearest poison control center. Keep this number easily accessible in case of emergency. If you know or suspect that your dog has ingested a specific poison, call the poison control center for the proper antidote. You can then relay this information to your veterinarian. If you do not know what the dog has ingested, call your veterinarian and describe the symptoms.

Common symptoms of poisoning are stomach pains, howling, whimpering, vomiting, diarrhea, convulsions, tremors, and labored breathing. Many poisons are fatal if not treated quickly. If you know the type of poison, your veterinarian may be able to save your dog by inducing vomiting or diarrhea, by pumping its stomach, or by neutralizing the poisons with appropriate medications.

One of the most common poisons ingested by dogs is rodent poison (these are usually blood anticoagulants). Symptoms include blood in the vomit, stool, and urine, and nose bleeding. Such poisoning can quickly prove fatal, and a veterinarian can help only if the dog has ingested a small amount of the poison.

Some pesticides are extremely poisonous. Store all pesticides away safely and keep dogs away from treated plants for at least two weeks after spraying. Poisoning results in diarrhea, cramps, shortness of breath, and dizziness.

Another common cause of poisoning is antifreeze. Dogs seem to love its taste. Although antifreeze itself is not poisonous, the dog's body converts it into several toxic substances that can lead to irreversible kidney damage and eventual death. If you see your dog drink antifreeze, immediately take the dog to your veterinarian.

Although not poisonings, bee and wasp stings can cause an irritating swelling, trembling, and circulatory failure. If your dog is stung in the throat area, swelling can suffocate the dog. Bring it immediately to your veterinarian.

Nursing A Sick Dog

You should be able to perform several procedures if your dog becomes ill. First learn the proper

Ailments and Illnesses

It is best to have two people take a Sheltie's temperature. One person can hold and calm the dog, while the other gently lifts the tail and carefully inserts a stubby thermometer into the rectum.

way to hold your dog, for you yourself may need to perform various medical procedures.

Lay the dog's head in the crook of your arm and hold it firmly, leaving your other arm free. While you do this, be sure to talk quietly to your Sheltie to help calm and reassure it.

The second procedure is taking your dog's temperature, for which you will need a regular rectal thermometer and some KY or petroleum jelly. Because you take the dog's temperature rectally, you may need someone to help you.

The normal body temperature of an adult Shetland sheepdog is between 100.5° and 101.5°F (38° to 38.6°C). The temperature is slightly higher in younger dogs and slightly lower in older ones. If your dog is placid, simply shake the mercury below 100°F (37.7°C), lubricate the thermometer with KY or petroleum jelly, lift the dog's tail, and slip the thermometer in. You can remove it after two or three minutes. If your dog is restless, have someone else calm it and hold its head firmly as previously described. Then lift its tail and insert the thermom-

eter. A restless dog may have an elevated temperature of a degree or so; however, increased temperatures of several points are usually a cause for alarm. Wash the thermometer in *cold* water when you are done. Taking your dog's temperature enables you to determine if it has a fever or hypothermia (subnormal temperature), which may be a symptom of poisoning.

You should also learn to take your dog's pulse. It is best to feel the pulse on the inside of the front paw or of the thigh on the heart side. An adult Sheltie has a pulse rate of 75 to 95 beats per minute, while in younger dogs the pulse is slightly quicker. In a calm, healthy Sheltie, the pulse is strong and steady. A weak pulse may indicate poisoning, while an irregular, pounding pulse is a symptom of fever or infection.

Finally, it is extremely important that a sick dog take all of its prescribed medicine. If you are lucky, your dog will readily accept any form of medicine, either straight from your hand or mixed with its food. However, if your dog does not take medicine willingly, you must administer it another way.

Powdered medications can be mixed with water and, like liquid medications, drawn into a syringe without a needle on it. Open the lips on the side of your dog's mouth near its molars. While loosely holding the dog's muzzle shut, let the liquid flow slowly into the space between the molars. Allow your dog time to swallow, until all of the liquid is taken. *Never* squirt the liquid into the mouth. This can cause coughing, resistance, and needless anxiety.

Your dog may object to taking pills or capsules. If the dog refuses to take a pill, put it inside some hamburger or other meat. Make sure your dog swal-

There are several color varieties of Shetland sheepdogs including: top left: tricolor; top right: golden sable; bottom left: blue merle; bottom right: mahogany sable.

lows all the medicine. Some dogs very cleverly hide a pill in the mouth and spit out the dose when the owner's back is turned.

If all other efforts fail, you may have to force your dog to swallow a pill. Hold the dog's upper jaw and, exerting mild pressure, raise its head. This should cause the dog's mouth to open. Quickly place the pill on the back of its tongue, hold its mouth closed, and tilt its head upward, and rub the dog's throat in a downward direction. This will force your dog to swallow the pill.

You will almost certainly need help if you must administer a suppository. Be sure to wear a disposable plastic glove for hygienic reasons. Have your assistant hold the dog with an arm across its chest and insert the suppository as far into the anus as possible.

When the Time Comes to Say Goodbye

For a dog owner whose pet has been truly loved, the most difficult time is when that devoted friend becomes terminally ill and will soon die. While modern veterinary medicine has numerous ways of extending the life of your pet, you must also be aware that no dog will live forever. In some cases veterinary care may be doing other than extending a dog's life. If your dog should become terminally ill and is experiencing severe and constant pain, most medical attention it receives would not prolong life, but rather, it would prolong the dying process.

Euthanasia is the act by which a veterinarian can painlessly induce death, ending the suffering of a terminally ill animal. When you must make the painful decision of having your dog put to sleep, consider the animal's feelings as well as your own. This is never an easy choice, and it will probably be made only after deep soul-searching. A caring veterinarian will understand the choices you may have to make and will be supportive and open for discussion. But remember that the decision must be yours.

Use only a minimal amount of pressure to pry open the dog's jaws when administering a pill.

Place the pill in the back of the dog's mouth, but do not force it into the throat, which could cause the dog to choke.

A typical pose of a herding dog. Note how the eyes and fully erect ears relay the expressions of vigilance and attentiveness.

Breeding Shetland Sheepdogs

Breeding Objectives

The objectives of dog breeding should always be to produce and raise puppies that will uphold the quality of the physical characteristics and the temperament of the breed. There are, however, some unscrupulous breeders who seek only to make a quick dollar on inferior litters. It is also too true that reckless breeding will increase in proportion to the popularity of the breed. Unfortunately, the Shetland sheepdog is not an exception to the rule.

With the increased popularity of the Shetland sheepdog we are beginning to see the result of these unprincipled breeding practices. We are beginning to see changes in the Shelties' physical size. Mainly, there are a greater number of Shelties larger than 16 inches (40 cm) (the Standard's maximum height) at the shoulder. In addition, we are beginning to see an increase in Shelties with behavioral abnormalities. In the end, not only will these breeders ruin the reputation of the breed, but they will also increase the already heartbreaking number of unwanted dogs.

Serious breeders wish to improve their dogs through selective breeding with quality dogs from other well–run kennels. Their main goal is to develop a bloodline of their own, one strong in the qualities that best exemplify the Shetland Sheepdog Standard.

The Shetland Sheepdog Standard is a complete written description of the perfect Sheltie: how it should look, act, and move. Of course, no one has ever produced the perfect Sheltie, and most likely, no one ever will. However, the Standard is the goal for which serious breeders strive. The Shetland Sheepdog Standard that is used in the United States was prepared by the American Shetland Sheepdog Association, and approved by the American Kennel Club (AKC). Every breed recognized by the AKC has its own Standard by which it is judged at dog shows.

If individual breeders were to produce what they considered perfect Shelties, the breed would vary widely. Without standards, each breed would quickly lose its identity. Adherence to the Standard separates conscientious breeders from unscrupulous ones who are more concerned with profits than with the quality and well-being of their puppies.

Characteristics of the Shetland Sheepdog

The following descriptions are based on my interpretation of the AKC-approved Standard for Shetland sheepdogs. However, this is not necessarily the interpretation of dog show judges. If you plan to enter your Sheltie in a conformation competition, obtain a copy of the Shetland Sheepdog Standard from the AKC. Remember that if you enter your Sheltie in a show competition, only the

The skeletal structure of the Shetland sheepdog. Refer to this drawing when reviewing the standard. This will make it easier to understand how the various parts of the dog's anatomy blend into one another.

Breeding Shetland Sheepdogs

judges' interpretation of the Standard will decide the winners.

General Description: The Shetland Sheepdog is a small, alert, rough–coated, long–haired working dog. He must be sound, agile, and sturdy. The outline should be so symmetrical that no part appears out of proportion to the whole. Males should look masculine, while females should look feminine.

Size: The Shetland sheepdog should have a measurement of between 13 and 16 inches (32.5–40 cm)

at the shoulder. Shoulder height measurements are taken with the dog standing naturally with its forelegs perpendicular to the ground. The measurement is taken from the ground directly up the foreleg to the top of the shoulder blades.

Coat: Because the Sheltie was originally bred as a herding dog for the harsh climate of the Shetland Islands, its coat must be suited to keep out the weather. Shelties have a double coat, the outer consisting of long, straight, coarse hair, while the un-

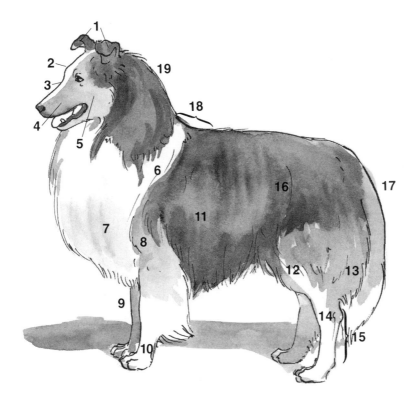

Conformation of the Shetland Sheepdog:
1. ears 2. skull 3. stop 4. muzzle 5. cheek 6. shoulder 7. chest 8. brisket 9. forequarters 10. front pastern 11. ribcage 12. stifle 13. hindquarters 14. hock 15. rear pastern 16. loin 17. tail 18. withers 19. neckline

Breeding Shetland Sheepdogs

dercoat is short and furry. It is the combination of these two coats that gives the Sheltie its full "stand-off" quality. The hair on the Sheltie's face, feet and the tips of its ears should be smooth. The mane of the Sheltie should be thick and full.

Because males should look more masculine, their mane and frills should be more abundant than those of a female. The hair on the forelegs and hindlegs are feathered, with the hind legs heavier than the forelegs on top but smooth below the hock joint (the joint equivalent to a backwards knee). The hair on a Sheltie's tail should also be thick and abundant. Any excess hair on the ears, feet, or hocks may be trimmed for the show ring.

Color: There are wide variations of color in Shelties. Black, blue merle, sable (ranging from golden to mahogany), marked with white and/or tan are all recognized color variations. (Blue merle consists of mottling of bluish-gray color on the face and back). Unacceptable color variations include rustiness in a black or blue coat; faded colors, conspicuous white spots or over 50% white.

Temperament: The Shetland sheepdog should exhibit the temperament one would associate with a herding dog. The dog should be intensely loyal, affectionate, and responsive to its owner or handler. The Standard allows for a Sheltie to be "reserved toward strangers"; however, the dog should show no signs of fear or cringing.

Head: The head, when viewed from the top, should "be a long, blunt wedge tapering slightly from ears to nose." The nose must always be black. The top of the skull is flat, without a prominent nuchal crest (the knotlike bone structure at the top of the skull). The cheeks of the Sheltie are flat and should smoothly curve into a "well-rounded muzzle." The muzzle should be the same length as the skull with the balance point at the inner corner of the eye when viewed from the side. The flattened line along the top of the Sheltie's skull should be parallel to the flat top of the muzzle, but on a higher plane due to the "presence of a slight but definite stop." The under jaw should be deep and well developed. It is rounded at the chin and extends to

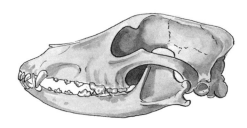

The skull of the Sheltie should resemble a long and tapered wedge, tapering slightly from ears to nose. The top of the skull is flat. The lower jaw is well developed and rounded at the chin.

the base of the nostril. A Sheltie's jaws are clean and powerful. When its lips are tight, the upper and lower lip meet and create a smooth seal all the way around. The teeth should be level and evenly spaced, with the dog having a "scissor" bite.

Eyes: A Sheltie's eyes are medium size and have dark, almond-shaped rims. The eyes must be dark. (Blue merle eyes are permissible only in blue merles). The eyes are set at a slight angle into the skull.

Ears: This breed has small and supple ears with the tips breaking forward. The ears are located high on the skull and carried about three-quarters erect. When resting, the Sheltie will fold its ears lengthwise and throw them back into the frill.

Expression: The basic shape and contour of the head, along with the location and positioning of its eyes and ears, all combine to produce the Sheltie's expression. Under normal conditions, the expression should be "alert, gentle, intelligent, and questioning." In the presence of a stranger, the expression should be one of watchfulness and caution; however, there should be no sign of fear.

Neck: Shelties have a muscular neck that should be arched, and long enough to carry its head proudly.

Body: The body should appear moderately long as measured from the shoulder joint to the ischium

Breeding Shetland Sheepdogs

(the rearmost extremity of the pelvic bone). The long appearance of the body is actually due to the proper breadth and angles of the shoulder and hindquarters. While the back of the Sheltie should be comparatively short, it must be level and well–muscled. A Shetland sheepdog has a deep chest with the brisket reaching to the back point of the elbow. Its ribs should be well–sprung but flattened at the lower half; this allows for the free movement of the foreleg and shoulder. The abdomen of the Sheltie should be tucked up fairly well, even though its coat may give the abdomen an appearance of being flat or rounded out.

Forequarters: When starting at the withers (the highest point of the shoulder), the shoulder blade should slope downward and forward, at a 45–degree angle to the shoulder joints. At the very top of the shoulders, the withers are separated only by the vertebrae, but they should slope outward at an angle sufficient to allow for the spring of the ribs. The upper arm should join the shoulder blade at a 90–degree angle. The elbow joint should be located midway between the withers and the ground. When viewed from any angle, the forelegs of the Sheltie must appear straight, muscular, clean and strong–boned. The pasterns (back of the foreleg) should appear strong, flexible, and sinewy.

Feet (Front and Hind): The feet are oval with well–arched toes that fit tightly together. A Sheltie has deep, tough pads and hard, strong nails on its feet.

Hindquarters: There should be a slight arch at the loins, and the croup (highest point of the rump) should gradually slope to the rear. The hipbone should be set at a 30–degree angle to the spine. The Sheltie should possess a broad and muscular thigh, and the thighbone should be set into the pelvis at a right angle (this corresponds to the angle made by the shoulder blade and the upper arms of the forelegs). The stifle bones (which join the hind leg and the body) should be "distinctly angled at the stifle joint." The overall length of the stifle bones should be equal to or slightly longer than the thighbone. The hock joint (the next joint below the stifle) should be angular and sinewy with good, strong bones and ligaments. The hock should be short and, like the foreleg, should be straight when viewed from all angles. Dewclaws should be removed.

Tail: The tail should be long enough that when it is laid along the back edge of the hind legs, the last vertebra will touch the hock joint. When the tail is at rest, it should be carried straight down or at a slight upward curve. When alert, the Sheltie will normally lift its tail; however, it should not curve forward and over its back.

Gait: When trotting, the Shetland sheepdog should give one the impression of "effortless speed and smoothness." The proper trot will show no signs of jerkiness, stiffness, or an up–and–down motion. The rear legs should appear to be the driving force, and the line on which it runs must be straight and true. If all the angulation, musculature, and ligamenta are correct, the rear legs of the trot-

The musculature of the Shetland sheepdog. Herding dogs require well-developed muscles to properly perform their duties.

ting Sheltie will reach well under its body, and then retract smoothly, propelling the dog forward. Proper "reach of stride" of the forelegs of the Sheltie is likewise dependent upon the proper angulation, musculature, and ligamenta of the forequarters. In addition, the proper reach of stride will be achieved only if the dog has the correct width of chest and construction of the rib cage. When trotting, the front feet should be lifted only enough to clear the ground when the legs swing forward. When viewing the dog from the front, both the forelegs and hind legs should be perpendicular to the ground when the dog is walking. When trotting, the legs should become angled inward, and when running swiftly, the "feet are brought so far inward toward center line of body that the tracks left show two parallel lines of footprints actually touching a center line at their inner edges." When moving, the Sheltie should not cross its feet or throw its weight from side to side.

Deviations from Breed Characteristics

As previously indicated, the Standard is a written description of the "perfect" Shetland sheepdog. Because perfect dogs do not exist, any Sheltie judged in terms of the Standard will have "faults." Most of these are difficult to detect in a puppy; as the puppy grows, however, deviations become more evident.

A fault is anything that negatively affects your Sheltie's appearance, temperament, or movement. Shyness, timidity, nervousness, stubbornness, snappiness, or ill temper are all undesirable traits in a Shetland sheepdog. Physical faults include: heights above or below the desired range, flat or short coats, lack of undercoat, color deviations, too-angled head, too prominent stop, prominent nuchal crest, domed skull, shallow under jaw, overshot or undershot jaw, missing or crooked teeth, poor eye color or position, ears set too low, hound

ears, feet turned in or out, or any deviation from the Standard measurements.

Remember that these faults apply only to bench competitions; they do not prevent the dog from competing in obedience or herding competitions.

A judge must separate winners from losers in the breeding ring. Therefore, if your Sheltie should prove to have a major fault, do not vent your disappointment on your dog. Be assured that your Sheltie is a diligent and hard worker that would do almost anything you may ask of it. Above all, remember that whether inside or outside of the ring, *your* opinion is the only one that matters to your Sheltie.

Breeding Your Female Sheltie

As I have previously mentioned, there is really only one reason why anyone should breed a dog. That reason is to produce a quality litter with the intention of improving the breed. If you are considering breeding your Sheltie to make some money, think again. Raising puppies requires time, space, and hard work, as well as a substantial investment of money. Yet, for all this, rarely does it return a profit.

The responsibilities of a dog breeder are numerous. Even before the dog is bred, the breeder must visit prospective stud dogs and spend a lot of time researching pedigrees and studying genetics. The breeder must keep the female dog in top breeding condition, help sustain her through the entire pregnancy, and then help her during delivery and raising the puppies. Once born, the puppies will need to be housed, fed, groomed, housebroken, and taken for all their veterinary care until good homes can be found for them.

If you are truly interested in breeding quality Shelties, and are not discouraged by the amount of responsibility you will have to undertake, then contact an experienced breeder. A professional can help you either breed your dog, or teach you the

Breeding Shetland Sheepdogs

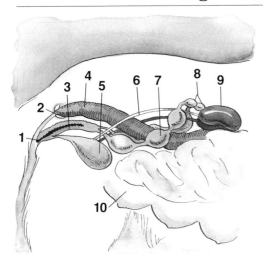

The reproductive organs of the female Sheltie:
1. vagina 2. anus 3. uterus 4. rectum 5. bladder 6. ureter 7. developing embryo 8. ovaries 9. kidney 10. teat

taining a list of available stud dogs from your Shetland Sheepdog Club, you should make appointments to visit as many of the breeders as possible. While visiting, keep in mind that you will be selecting the dog that best compliments your female. You should study each dog for its conformation to the breed Standard. Then you should ask to see the dog's pedigree. The pedigree will show you if there are any champions in the stud dog's bloodline. Although breeding your female to a champion stud dog is a good start, you should place much greater emphasis on the overall quality of the dog's bloodlines.

In selecting a dog with the correct conformation, you will once again need to familiarize yourself with the breed Standard. Choose a dog that best exemplifies the Standard's descriptions. Avoid a dog with faults similar to those of your female. In

principles of dog breeding. Under no circumstances should an amateur deliberately breed a female Sheltie.

Once you have an understanding of the principles of breeding, seek the advice of your local Shetland Sheepdog Club. This group is a valuable source of information and can help you find a suitable stud dog. The following is a summary of the information you need before breeding your Sheltie. Remember that this is only a summary, and not an all-inclusive guide to breeding. Once again, I urge you to learn from a reputable breeder as much as possible before you breed your female Sheltie.

Choosing a Mate

Selecting the proper mate for your female Sheltie will involve some lessons in genetics. After ob-

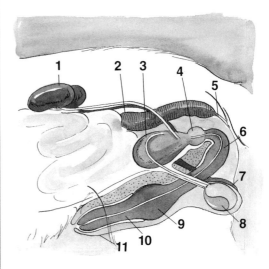

The reproductive organs of the male Sheltie:
1. kidneys 2. rectum 3. bladder 4. prostate 5. anus 6. urethra 7. scrotum 8. testes 9. bulb 10. penis 11. sheath

Breeding Shetland Sheepdogs

breeding, the objective is to improve the female's bloodline by eliminating her faults. Obviously, the best way to do this is to breed your female to a stud who has strong qualities wherever she has faults.

In some instances, your choice of stud dog may be influenced by the type of dog you intend to raise. For instance, if you wish to breed for show stock, you would want to find a male with a good show record. If you plan to raise a litter that will be sold exclusively as house dogs, you should pay special attention to the temperament of the stud dog. After all, you want house dogs to have a good disposition and be friendly toward their owners.

Once you choose a stud dog, you will have to agree with the owner on a stud fee. Naturally, champion stud dogs command a higher price than pet–quality animals. Many times the stud dog's owner takes the pick of the litter instead of money, but this must be agreed upon ahead of time.

If you have difficulty selecting a stud dog, the breeder from whom you purchased your female can offer invaluable assistance.

Prior to mating, introduce your female to the male. Be sure to keep both dogs on a leash in case you have to separate them quickly.

The male dog will mount the female from behind. You may have to hold your female still should she be excessively nervous.

When Is the Female Ready?

The age at which you can first breed your female is between 16 and 18 months. However, it is usually best to wait until her second or third "season." It is important to wait until she is mature enough to cope with the physical and mental demands of a litter.

Before your female's estrus, bring her to the veterinarian to be checked for worms and for a booster shot, if she has not recently had one. Also make sure she is neither overweight nor under-weight.

When her season is near, check her daily for the swelling of her vulva and the appearance of color. The best time to breed a female (the time at which the chance of conception is highest) is from 9 to 14 days after the first signs of color. The female is ready for the mating when the color changes from dark red to yellow.

When the swelling and color first appear, make an appointment with the owner of the stud dog to bring the female for mating. (The female is always brought to the male.) Once mating has taken place, do not attempt to separate the dogs if they are still coupled, for this can cause injury. Once the dogs

Breeding Shetland Sheepdogs

If the dogs have trouble separating after mating, they may wind up back to back. If this happens you must be careful when separating them so that neither dog becomes injured.

are separated, remove the female and put her in her cage or in your car. Do not allow her to urinate for about a half hour after breeding.

Remember that although your female has been bred, male dogs will still be attracted to her. Guard her carefully during the next week or so until she is definitely out of season.

The Birth of Puppies

Once the mating of your female is completed, it is time to begin getting ready for the most wonderful moments you will have as a breeder—the birth of her puppies. Once again, it is important to thoroughly prepare both yourself and your Sheltie for this event, so that there will be as little confusion as possible when it is her time to give birth. The less confusion there is, the less stressful it will be on her, and the more enjoyable it will be for you.

Guard her carefully until she is fully out of season. This completed, it is time to return to your normal routines and make sure she gets her daily exercise. Your Sheltie will have to be in good physical condition for the duration of her pregnancy.

You should be able to tell if the mating was successful within five to six weeks, as her abdomen begins to swell. At this point you can switch her over to a special whelping diet—in accordance with your veterinarian's instructions. As the next several weeks pass, your female Sheltie will most likely require an increasing amount of food. After about seven weeks you can start to cut down on her exercise.

With the big day only a few weeks away, it is time to introduce your female to her whelping box. This box can be either handmade or purchased. If you make it by hand, use the same rules for materials as you would with a sleeping box (see section entitled "Equipment and Accessories," page 14). You will have to use your best judgment when figuring out the dimensions of the whelping box. It must be big enough for the mother to lie down and stretch out, but small enough to keep the puppies from wandering away and becoming chilled. Put the box in a warm, quiet, draft–free spot and line it with a thick layer of newspapers covered by a clean blanket and some cloths that can be easily changed.

Maintain the temperature around the box between 70° and 80°F (21°–27°C) for at least five weeks after the puppies are born. By then they should be able to maintain their own body temperature. If the puppies are born during the winter, you may find it necessary to use heat lamps or electric heaters as an additional heat source. When using either heat lamps or electric heaters, it is important that you test them thoroughly, and be sure they are not placed either too close or too far away from the box. If you choose to use any other type of heater, make sure it is safe and will not harm the female or her puppies.

The gestation period of a Shetland sheepdog is usually nine weeks; your female will let you know when whelping time is near. She will become restless and wander in and out of her box. She will begin to lose the hair around her breasts. This is perfectly normal and it serves to enable the newborn puppies to easily find their source of nourishment. As the big day draws nearer the female's breasts will swell with milk, and the nipples will darken in color. If for some reason the female does not lose the hair around her breasts, you should carefully cut it short with a pair of scissors. This will prevent matting and make it easier for the puppies to feed.

At this time, remove all distractions from around your Sheltie. Only you should be present at this time. Having an audience or noisy children nearby will worry your dog. Be sure you do not disturb her. Give her plenty of room and stay nearby, speaking softly to calm her. Eventually she will settle in her box and begin her labor, which includes heavy panting followed by visible contractions. Soon the first puppy will appear at the vulva and will slide out with the contraction.

The mother Sheltie will actually take care of the entire birth process, and in most cases you will be needed only if there are complications. When the puppy is completely out, the mother should immediately tear open the amniotic sac and shred the umbilical cord, using her teeth. She will then begin to clean the puppy by licking it. While she is licking the puppy she may also rub her muzzle along the underside and sides of the newborn pup. This serves to massage and stimulate the puppy to begin breathing. If the mother attempts to eat the afterbirth, allow it, for this is perfectly natural. The afterbirth is high in nutrients, and eating it will promote the production of milk, as well as encourage further labor for the birth of the next puppy.

The puppies should be born at about half–hour intervals. The average Sheltie litter is about seven puppies, so it will take about seven to eight hours from the start of labor until the last puppy is born. If you have an unusually large litter, you may have to help the mother feed her young. A Sheltie mother has only ten teats. If the litter is larger than that, you will have to bottle-feed the additional puppies. In doing this, you will prevent the mother from being overburdened. Commercial milk supplements are available at most pet shops.

Usually a female Sheltie will give birth without any problems, but on rare occasions there may be complications. A few Shelties seem to lack the basic maternal instincts. While the cause of this is unknown, it is generally assumed that it is a result of generations of domestication. If you experience such an occurrence, it will be your responsibility to finish the delivery. Once the newborn has emerged from the mother you must firmly pinch the cord in the middle with your fingers. If you can not pinch hard enough, you may have to use a pair of pliers. Next, cut the cord a few inches from the puppy's belly, using a pair of scissors. When you open the amniotic sac, begin near the puppy's nose and remove the sac from around the puppy's body. Gently open the puppy's mouth, and carefully remove any mucus that may be obstructing the breathing passages. Finally, rub a warm towel, without exerting too much pressure, back and forth across the puppy's chest for about 15 minutes. This will stimulate its breathing.

Care Of Puppies

So there they are—these cute, soft bundles of wrinkles, barely resembling their mother. Yet they will grow to be proud members of the Shetland breed. When Sheltie pups are born, they cannot see or hear. However, a well–developed sense of smell helps them locate their mother's teats.

During the first few weeks of their lives, the puppies will be totally taken care of by their mother. She will nurse them, clean them, and even lick up their excretion in order to keep the whelping box clean. You will merely have to assist her by changing the box lining whenever it is necessary. Enjoy this time while you can, because it doesn't last long. Once the puppies are four weeks old, you will have more than enough responsibilities to keep your hands full.

By the fourth week, the puppies' eyes are completely open, their hearing is more acute, and they are much more aware of their environment. They are also starting to look a little more like their parents. You can now begin to wean them. Weaning

Breeding Shetland Sheepdogs

Shortly after the birth of the puppies, the mother Sheltie will settle down and nurse her litter.

means that the puppies stop depending on their mother for food and begin to eat on their own. Begin weaning as soon as possible, for the mother's milk supply quickly runs short of the demand.

The weaning process can be a little difficult if you do not have a good technique. The easiest method, I have learned, is to purchase a high–quality commercial puppy food and soften it with hot water. Mix the food and water until it is lukewarm and of a thin consistency. Place the food in a large flat dish and put the puppies around it. Dip your finger into the food, and smear some on the end of each puppy's nose. To your delight, they will stick out their little pink tongues and clean the end of their little black noses. After this they usually get the message and quickly sniff at the plate, and then eat from it. Once the puppies are eating on their own, you can begin to decrease the amount of water you mix with their food. Gradually cut back until the puppies are eating dry food. Once they have reached this stage, you can begin to add fresh meat or canned puppy food to their diet.

When the puppies are about six or seven weeks old, take them to your veterinarian for a series of temporary shots. Also bring a few stool samples so the veterinarian can check for worms. Many puppies become infested with roundworms contracted from their mothers. These worms can be harmful if left untreated. If worming is needed, medicate the puppies as directed by your veterinarian.

Eventually the puppies will begin to wander about and explore your house. Now you will have to "puppy-proof" your home. You will have to remove, or keep out of reach, anything that may be harmful if eaten or chewed. Once you have removed all harmful objects, you need to keep the puppies' little jaws busy chewing on something else. To strengthen their jaw muscles and teeth, you can give them suitably sized rawhide bones or teething toys specifically designed for dogs.

Like most puppies, Shelties are naturally curious; do not keep them from human contact, especially with members of its human family. If a puppy tends to be shy, increase the amount of time you spend with it until it no longer fears people.

Once the puppies are seven weeks old, they should really begin to resemble their parents. Unfortunately, for the emotionally attached breeder, it is also the time when puppies must leave each other and find new homes. You can contact your Shetland Sheepdog Club about potential buyers and finding the puppies good homes. Naturally, you will be very concerned about the quality of homes your puppies receive. Do not be afraid to ask prospective buyers about their homes and their views on dog ownership. Remember the questions asked of you when you purchased your Sheltie. Now you can understand the breeder's concern for the puppy's well–being. Perhaps, for any number of reasons, you will decide to keep one or more of the puppies. Just make sure you have the time, space, and money it takes to give all of your Shelties the best home possible.

Dog Shows and Exhibitions

A purebreed such as the Shetland sheepdog may be entered in any dog show or obedience competition. These licensed shows are conducted under rules established by the AKC. The term "dog show" usually refers to a bench competition in which a Shetland sheepdog is judged on appearance, physique, bearing, and temperament. In these events, a dog is judged strictly on how it conforms to the Standard for that particular breed as compared to all the other dogs that are entered in the competition.

At obedience trials a Sheltie is judged entirely on performance in a series of exercises. These exercises, chosen beforehand by the AKC, are based upon any work the dog may be required to do. The exercises to be performed are based on the dog's experience in the obedience ring and may include heel on leash, heel free, recall, long sit, retrieve on flat or over high jump, broad jump, scent discrimination, or a signal exercise.

Another type of exhibition sponsored by the AKC is the field trial. However, these competitions are designed for hunting dogs, such as spaniels or retrievers. Most of the events in a field trial are designed to simulate actual hunting conditions, and as such, make it impossible for a herding dog such as the Sheltie to compete fairly.

There is good news on the way, however, for owners of herding dogs. In the United States, there have been herding competitions run by many local clubs and national herding dog associations, but they have never been conducted under AKC–established rules. Recently, however, the AKC has taken up the task of establishing and putting in writing a formal set of rules and regulations for herding competitions. At the time of publication of this book, the rules had not been completed; however, it is hoped that they will be finished and in effect sometime early in 1990.

Because bench competitions, obedience competitions, and herding trials each have a different format, you should attend them to learn more about judging. Also, these competitions offer dog owners a wide variety of helpful information. Manufacturers of dog food and other pet products often attend and sometimes display their merchandise. You will also be able to exchange tips with other dog owners and breeders. Often the judges advise owners on the care and grooming of their dogs.

If you wish to enter your dog in a show, check with your local Shetland Sheepdog Club. They can advise you about the event, help you obtain and complete the application form, and inform you of the entry fee. Prior to the show, you must supply the judges with your dog's pedigree, certificate of health, and an International Certificate of Immunization.

Whether you enter your Sheltie or not, attending a dog show is a rewarding and educational experience. If you do decide to enter your dog, do not count on its winning or achieving a good score. Remember that dog show judges are very strict. Your Sheltie may not meet their interpretation of the Standard. If this is the case, just enjoy the show and the experience of owning a purebreed dog.

Basic and Advanced Training

Like almost all of the herding dogs, Shetland sheep-dogs are relatively easy to train. This is because the hundreds of years of shepherd–dog relationships have imprinted the Sheltie with an innate willingness to learn. For this reason, you can begin to train a Sheltie at a much earlier age than many other breeds. In addition, if you conduct your training program properly, you will be able to keep your Sheltie puppy's attention for a longer period of time, thus leading to quicker learning.

Bear in mind that this chapter does not describe all the skills a Sheltie can learn. In fact, I believe that if you have the time, patience, and energy, you can teach your Sheltie an endless number of skills. You must, however, be able to communicate your ideas to your eager student.

Why Dogs Learn

Dogs are pack animals. Because they hunt and live as a group, dogs must learn to coexist in order to survive. This coexistence depends on ranking order. Each dog has a place in the ranking order, usually based on strength and experience. In the pack, all dogs submit to a dog of higher authority. Similarly, a domesticated dog submits only to a higher ranking authority.

Through training, a puppy learns that you are the authority and that the other members of your family rank higher than it does. In addition to establishing ranking order, training teaches your puppy the rules of your house. Teaching a puppy actions and behaviors that are not instinctive takes patience, understanding, and love. You must be consistent and authoritative, yet must never lose your temper. Try to understand that human ways are unfamiliar to your Sheltie puppy, but that it is eager to learn. Your puppy depends on you to find the proper way to teach it. Once you find the right method, your puppy will respond eagerly and joyfully.

Basic Rules of Training

Each time you hold a training session for your Sheltie, consider the following points:

1) You and your family must be consistent. All household members must decide what is permitted and what is prohibited. Once you have taught your dog a lesson, never allow it to do the contrary without reprimand.

2) Be authoritative. Although your dog must learn that you are in charge, *never* do this by using physical force. Shelties can quickly learn hand signals, and they can understand sounds. Therefore, deliver all visual and verbal commands clearly and unmistakably. Because dogs understand tones better than words, be sure your reprimands are always sharp and firm while your praise is always calm and friendly.

3) Run each training session with an atmosphere conducive to learning. Have your dog perform the lesson where there are as few distractions as possible. In addition, never attempt to teach a puppy anything if you are in a bad mood. This will only confuse the puppy and make learning harder.

4) Do not attempt to teach your dog more than one concept in a single training session, and never move on to another concept until your dog has mastered the previous lesson. Puppies, like people, learn at their own pace and should never be rushed.

5) Praise your dog generously after it has performed correctly. Verbal praise and petting or scratching behind the ears will make your Sheltie an eager learner. Although it is commonplace for trainers to reward their pupil with food, I personally feel that it is not necessary. A dog that has just eaten may not necessarily perform to your commands when all it has to gain is more food. Your puppy should learn to perform correctly with the incentive of your enthusiastic praise.

6) Punish disobedience immediately. Because a puppy has a very short memory, never hesitate to reprimand it. If your puppy chews your slipper (which you should remember not to leave within its

Basic and Advanced Training

reach), do not punish it unless you catch it in the act. You should certainly reprimand an adult dog that knows better after showing it the slipper, providing it leaves a shred of evidence. Punishment should take the form of verbal disapproval. In extreme conditions you may place the dog in its cage after verbally reprimanding it.

7) Begin working with your puppy the day you bring it home. Hold two or three sessions a day, and continue these sessions as long as your puppy shows interest. By limiting your sessions to 10 or 15 minutes each, you will provide sufficient teaching without boring your dog. Your puppy may need two weeks or longer to begin to understand some of your commands, so do not neglect your training. Shelties must learn these basic lessons at a very young age.

While Shelties might be considered "lap" dogs, they should be taught to stay off furniture.

Training a Puppy

As previously mentioned, training begins the day you bring your puppy home. The longer you wait, the more difficult it will be for your puppy to learn. First teach your Sheltie its name. If you always address your puppy by name, you will be amazed at how fast it will learn this lesson. Make sure your Sheltie does not hear nicknames; this will confuse it, and it will not respond when called.

Another important lesson is the meaning of "no." Your puppy will probably have to begin learning this lesson its first day at home. As your puppy first explores your home, it will probably do something wrong. When it does, tell it "no" in a sharp, firm tone that shows you are serious. If your puppy refuses to listen, pick it up and place it in its cage. *Never* hit your puppy, either with your hand or with a rolled newspaper, for this will make your puppy hand–shy. Using a cage will simplify training. In addition, as you will see in the next section, it will also speed the process of housebreaking.

Housebreaking Your Puppy

Many people choose to get older dogs rather than a puppy because they think that housebreaking a puppy is too difficult. However, if you choose the proper method for you, and take all the right steps, you can avoid a lot of the drudgery associated with housebreaking.

Outdoor Training: Most puppies will find it necessary to relieve themselves as many as six times a day. From the moment you bring your puppy home, you should begin its training. First, before you bring the puppy indoors, walk it in the area you have chosen for it to eliminate. Give the puppy time to become acquainted with its surroundings, and give it ample time to excrete. Remember to praise your dog each time after it eliminates. Praising your puppy each time increases the chances of its repeating the act properly.

Another step you should take is to bring your puppy outdoors after meals. When a puppy's stom-

Basic and Advanced Training

ach is full, it will exert pressure on the bladder and colon, so it is best not to wait too long after mealtime. If you continue to bring your puppy to the same area and continue to praise it each time, the puppy should begin to seek out this area on its own.

Finally, you should always take your puppy for its last walk of the day as late as possible. Even though it may be late, remain patient and allow your puppy to take its time. By doing this you increase your chances of making it through the night and avoiding unpleasant morning surprises.

Indoor Training: There are two housebreaking methods should you decide to use an "indoor" technique. One method is paper training and the other involves the use of a cage.

For paper training you should spread several layers of newspapers in an area that you choose beforehand where the dog is to urinate and defecate. The place you choose should be in an easy-to-clean area, like a kitchen or bathroom. It is also important not to put the papers too close to the puppy's eating and sleeping areas. Dogs will try to keep these areas clean and will not mess near them. At first you can confine your puppy to this room until it voids. If the puppy goes on the paper, then remove the top sheets of paper and place new, clean papers under the formerly bottom sheets. By doing this, you will be leaving the scent from the bottom papers exposed so that the puppy can relocate the area easier and repeat the act.

If the puppy should miss the paper at first, attempt to get the scent of the dog's urine onto a sheet of paper and place it on top of the other sheets. Then thoroughly clean the area where the puppy did go. It is important that the puppy seek out its scent on the papers and not find it on the floor, where it will repeat its action.

Cage training is my choice for indoor housebreaking, for I find it much easier and faster than paper training. The cage becomes the puppy's "house," and (fortunately for humans), dogs instinctively need to keep their houses clean.

When the puppy first encounters the cage, it may be wary. To make it feel more comfortable,

Housebreaking can be made easier if you put some of your puppy's scent on the paper being used. A puppy will rely more on smell than sight to locate the area where it should relieve itself.

feed it or give it a toy to play with inside the cage. After you have confined the puppy to its cage a few times with its excreta, it will quickly learn to "hold it in" until you let it out of the cage. This means that after you take the puppy out of its cage, you must bring it outdoors immediately. Establish a time schedule for taking your puppy out of its cage. Wait for it to relieve itself before bringing it back indoors. As your trust in your puppy grows, you can let it out for longer and longer periods, until eventually you can leave the cage door open at all times, provided you take the dog outside as scheduled.

While many people cringe at the thought of confining a dog to a cage, I would like to assure you that there is nothing to worry about. Prior to domestication, dogs had always been cave-dwelling animals. Instinctively, the modern dog finds security in any cavelike structure, once it becomes familiar with it. If you choose to use a cage, you will find that your dog will actually prefer to sleep there, and will return on its own. Remember that if your dog did not enjoy the cage it would never go in voluntarily. Should you decide to use a cage, you can also use it as a sleeping box and a traveling

Basic and Advanced Training

crate. In addition to offering safety and comfort, the cage is useful when you are unable to supervise the puppy.

Regardless of the housebreaking method you choose, always take your Sheltie for its last walk of the day as late as possible. This can help to minimize any late night "accidents." No matter how careful you are, however, it is almost inevitable that an "accident" will happen sooner or later.

If you should discover that while you slept your puppy could no longer control itself, it will do no good to administer any punishment. Puppies have very short memories, so if you do not catch your dog in the act, or shortly afterward, a scolding will only confuse it. Should you catch your Sheltie in the act, scold it with a sharp "No!" Then you can put it in its cage. Never spank your puppy, for it serves no purpose. And never put your puppy's nose in the mess. Not only is this an unsanitary thing to do, but it will only upset the puppy, and give you one more thing to clean up.

Being Alone

A puppy must learn early that it will be left alone on occasion. You must teach it to behave properly while you are away, for a poorly trained puppy can cause great damage.

To accustom your puppy to being alone, leave it in a familiar room. Then go into another room where the puppy can neither see nor hear you. Stay there for a short while and then return; if your puppy has done anything wrong, reprimand it. Gradually increase the time you leave the dog in the room alone.

If you must leave before you can trust your puppy alone, lock it in its cage with food, water, and toys until you return. If you do not have a cage, lock it in a familiar room. Remove all tempting objects, including shoes, papers, and clothing. Make sure you leave the puppy its bed and an ample supply of food, water, and toys.

Do not leave a very young puppy alone in your yard, where there are too many uncontrollable factors. Children may tease the puppy, and other animals may be able to bother or hurt it.

No Begging Allowed

To some people, seeing a dog beg looks like a cute and innocent act. Unfortunately, begging is a bad habit for a puppy to develop, and it should never be condoned. Begging may start very innocently. You will be sitting down at the table, about to begin eating a thick steak, when you notice something out of the corner of your eye. It is your faithful puppy, waiting patiently nearby, staring at you with pleading eyes. Now is when most people make their big mistake. They will call the dog over and reward it with a table scrap. You would be amazed at how such a simple act could turn into a nasty habit. While having your Sheltie as a constant table companion may not bother you, it may bother others who are guests in your house.

If your Sheltie attempts to beg for scraps, you must scold it with a sharp "No!" and point away from the table and toward the puppy's cage or sleeping box. Within a few weeks, your puppy will learn to avoid the table during mealtimes.

Walking on a Leash

You should start to teach your puppy how to walk on a leash from the first day you bring it home. Before you even bring the puppy into your home, you will be taking it for a walk around your yard to let it relieve itself. Place a collar on the puppy,

There are few breeds that can match the elegance, expression, and beauty of Shetland sheepdogs.

Basic and Advanced Training

making sure it is neither too tight nor too loose. Attach a leash and take your puppy for its first walk. Hold the leash on your left side and use gentle persuasion to keep your puppy close to your leg. Do not allow the puppy to get under your feet, and do not let it run ahead of you. Remain patient. A Sheltie puppy's legs are very short, and it is not capable of tremendous speed. If your puppy falls behind, do not attempt to drag it forward. Use friendly words, patience, and a little bit of gentle force to keep your puppy in its proper walking position.

No Unnecessary Barking Allowed

Barking is one of the most common problems of canine behavior. It is, of course, a natural response for almost all dogs. Even though there may be numerous causes of barking, including behavioral problems, this section deals with some corrective approaches you can take to help break bad learned behaviors.

Barking is often the sign of alarm, and because of this, you may not want to curb any of your Sheltie's watchdog tendencies. It is therefore important to discover whether any of your dog's bad barking habits are an inherited problem or a learned behavior. Inherited problems are discussed in the section entitled, "Understanding the Shetland Sheepdog" (page 72).

A learned behavior, for example, is one where the dog barks upon hearing the command "speak." If a dog has been trained by getting food after it "speaks," then a dog may "speak" on its own in order to get a reward. This habit can be broken by

never giving a dog a reward after it is told to speak. This method is called extinction and relies on the trainer to repeat the command over and over, but never, ever giving the dog a reward (outside of a verbal praise and petting).

This type of training is normally very effective in stopping any bad learned behaviors (such as barking to get into or out of the house; barking in order to receive food or attention, etc.). But be warned. It may take a lot of time and patience to break such bad habits.

Simple Commands

The first commands to teach your sheepdog are "sit," "stay," "come," and "heel." Teach these commands using these words, and not phrases like "Come over here, Sparky." Your dog does not understand complete sentences, but rather relies on the command word, your tone, and your gesture. Do not try to teach your Sheltie these commands for long periods of time. It is better to train for short periods two or three times a day. Train before you feed the dog, because afterwards it may be sluggish. Also, make sure to walk the dog before training. To avoid distractions, train your puppy in a confined area without an audience.

Sit: Take your puppy into an isolated room and fit it with a collar and leash. Hold the leash with your right hand and place your left hand on the puppy's hindquarters. Then give the command "Sit!" or "Sit, Sparky!" in a firm voice, at the same time pressing gently and steadily on its hindquarters. Gently pull the leash upward to keep your puppy from lying down on the floor. Hold the dog in this position for a while. Do not allow it to jump back up.

Do not expect your Sheltie to master this command after the first training session. Repeat the procedure for the entire session or until the puppy begins to lose interest. Remember to praise its efforts each time it sits properly. If you repeat the procedure every day, your Sheltie will soon learn this command.

A little piece of Sheltie heaven. This puppy nibbles on his favorite treat while passing time on a summer day.

Basic and Advanced Training

While teaching the "sit" command, use one hand to gently push your Sheltie's hindquarters down. Simultaneously, use the other hand to hold the head upright with the aid of the leash.

Once your puppy has performed the "Sit" at least a couple of times in succession, remove the leash and give the command. If your dog has been properly trained, it will perform correctly. If not, remain patient and try again with the leash on.

If you want to use your Sheltie for herding, teach it to respond to a hand signal and to whistles as well. In the field your dog may be at a distance where it can see you but not hear you. This way your dog can understand your command even if noise prevents it from hearing you. In addition, the sharp sounds of whistles are easier than verbal commands for your dog to hear and interpret from a distance. Once your puppy has mastered the command, hold up either your hand or a single finger in a distinct gesture and say "Sit," making sure the dog can see the signal. Always use the word (or sound) and the gesture together so your dog connects the two.

Stay: This is a more difficult command to teach your puppy, for it will always want to be at your side. The "Stay" command orders your dog to remain still wherever it is. This command may someday save your dog's life.

In teaching your dog to "stay," first fit it with a leash and collar. Then run through the "Sit" procedure and follow it with the command "Stay." As you say this new command, raise your hand, palm toward the dog, like a police officer stopping traffic. Each time your dog attempts to stand up, reproach it with a sharp "No!"

Take up all the slack in the leash to hold your dog in place. Repeat the procedure until the dog appears to understand. Then remove the leash and repeat the command several times. Praise the dog each time it obeys. If it disobeys, reprimand it.

Continue this command until your Sheltie has repeated the act with regular success. Then, slowly back away from the dog, making sure to maintain eye contact. While you are moving backward, keep repeating the word "Stay." The verbal command should be accompanied by the proper hand gesture.

Before teaching the "stay" command, introduce your Sheltie to the proper hand signal.

Basic and Advanced Training

If your Sheltie attempts to follow, give it a loud, sharp "Stay!" If the dog continues to follow you, reprimand it. Of course a dog that stays when told deserves great praise. The "Stay" command is sometimes difficult for a devoted puppy to obey because it will always have the urge to be by your side.

Come: If you call out your puppy's name, it will probably race across the room to greet you. The trick to the "Come" command, however, is to have your Sheltie obediently come to you when something of greater interest is attracting its attention. "Come" is another command that can protect your dog from dangerous situations.

You should teach the command "Come" to your puppy right after "Sit" and "Stay." Start by running through the "Sit" and "Stay" procedures. Once it has "stayed" at a good distance, call the dog by name and follow with the command, "Sparky, come!" Accompany your words with a lively sound or gesture like clapping your hands or slapping your thighs. This will help to excite your dog into motion.

Your Sheltie will quickly associate the word "Come" with your movements. Praise it for responding correctly. If it does not respond to the command, put it on a long rope and let it wander off. Then slowly reel in the rope while repeating the word "Come!" Shower your dog with praise when it reaches you. Repeat this exercise several times; then try it without the rope again. Luckily, most Shelties never require this rope exercise.

Obedience Training

The obedience exercises are important for several reasons. Each of the exercises is a requirement for your dog to perform, should you enter it in an obedience competition. However, some of the lessons, such as "heeling" or "relinquishing an object," are important for all dogs to learn. They will allow you to properly handle your dog in awkward situations, and will help to reinforce your dog's understanding of the master/subordinate relationship.

Using Obedience Schools for Training

Contrary to popular belief, obedience schools are not schools for "wayward" dogs. Instead, they are where, in the proper atmosphere, your dog can learn all it must know to compete in shows. Even if you do not plan to enter your Sheltie in an obedience trial, these schools offer an enjoyable, interesting, and easy alternative to training your dog alone. These schools are run by experienced dog handlers, who can supply you with expert advice and invaluable training tips.

An older child in the family should be the one to take your Sheltie to obedience classes. This allows the child and dog to spend more time together. It also teaches your child how to care for a dog responsibly. Working with a dog at obedience

Involving your children in your puppy's obedience training and/or trials will help them learn the responsibilities of pet ownership.

Basic and Advanced Training

school will teach your child both greater self-respect and respect for the dog.

Check with your Shetland Sheepdog Club and the AKC for a reputable obedience school in your area. Before enrolling your dog, make sure the class suits your purpose. Most schools offer special classes for owners interested in showing their dogs, and others for amateurs. Remember that obedience schools can be costly, depending on the problems your dog presents.

Heeling

When your Sheltie heels properly, it will walk on your left with its head about the same distance forward as your knees. When you begin teaching your dog this lesson you will require the leash. Eventually your Sheltie must learn to "Heel" without the restraint of the leash.

To start, run through all the other commands your dog has mastered. This will give your dog extra confidence before you start this difficult lesson. Hold the end of the leash in your right hand, and grab about halfway toward the collar with your left hand. Begin a brisk walk (by your dog's standard) giving the sharp command "Heel!" or "Heel, Sparky!" Use your left hand to control and guide. With this new command, your dog may act rather unpredictably at first, but be patient.

If your dog lags behind, pull steadily on the leash to bring it even with your leg. Do not drag the dog forward or force it to obey your commands, for this will destroy the well–established learning atmosphere. If your dog runs forward, pull it back to your side and give the "Heel" command again. If you have difficulty getting your dog to perform correctly, run through the old "Sit" and "Stay" exercises. Whenever your dog responds correctly, praise it. When it reacts improperly, reprimand it immediately. When it has performed the "Sit" and "Stay" correctly, begin the "Heel" exercises again.

The "Heel" lesson is very difficult for a dog to learn, so take your time, be patient, and do not try

The proper "heeling" position. You should "choke up" on the leash for better control.

to teach your dog too quickly. Once your Sheltie has mastered the "Heel" on a leash, take it through a turning exercise. If it has trouble heeling while you turn, then take a shorter grip on the leash, and bring the dog closer to your side. Then repeat the command "Heel!" in a sharp tone, and gently persuade it to follow you by lightly pulling on the leash. As your Sheltie improves in this lesson, take it through a series of straight line, right turn, and left turn exercises. Once it has mastered turning, it is time to begin training with a slack leash.

Go through the heeling exercises with the leash exerting no pressure on your dog's collar. At the dog's first mistake, grasp the leash firmly and lead the dog steadily in the proper direction. When it performs correctly, remember to praise it.

When your dog has learned to walk correctly with a slack leash, remove the leash completely. If it has performed properly with a loose leash, you should be able to achieve the same results without

Basic and Advanced Training

it. Do not allow your Sheltie to regress into any bad habits. If the dog does not perform properly, then a verbal reprimand is needed. If you continue to have trouble, you will have to put the leash back on. Repeat the "Heel" lesson, then try again without the leash. If you repeat the lessons carefully, and have the exact same routine with and without the leash, your dog should eventually learn to heel properly. Always remember to praise a job well done. This will help to reinforce your Sheltie's good behavior.

Relinquishing an Object

Every good dog must learn to obediently give up any object, if its master so desires. Shelties are no exception. This lesson is important in teaching your dog its subordinate role.

Begin by giving your Sheltie a suitably sized piece of nonsplintering wood to hold in its teeth. Then command your dog to sit, praising it when it obeys. Using both hands, slowly pull the dog's jaws apart, while saying "Let Go!" in a strict and firm tone. If your dog begins to growl, give it a sharp "No!" Do not be afraid if your Sheltie growls. This is a dog's way of trying to establish its dominance, and a natural reaction to anyone who attempts to take away its prey. You must, however, make it clear to your Sheltie that you are the boss, and take the object away. Once your dog accepts you as a dominant force, it will give up the stick without any objection.

Lying Down

Have your dog assume a sitting position (which should be easy by now). Then slowly pull its front legs forward while saying "Down!" If your dog attempts to stand up, give it a sharp "No!" If pulling on its front legs does not work, then slowly pull them forward and push down on the dog's shoulders at the same time. While you do this give the command "Down!" Because you will have both hands occupied, you can carefully step on the leash to prevent the dog from returning to its feet. Keep

the dog in the lying position for about one minute. Gradually increase this time period as your dog progresses. When your dog has mastered this lesson, begin to move away. As you do this, you must maintain constant eye contact with your pupil. Whenever the dog attempts to stand up, repeat the command "Down!" in a firm, sharp tone. Repeat the lesson until you are satisfied with your Sheltie's performance.

Retrieving

Retrieving is an unusual act for any sheepdog to perform; however, you may be surprised at the number of Shelties who perform this feat as if it were instinctive. On the other hand, I have met several other Shelties that would attempt to "herd" a ball back to its owner by encircling it and barking rather than picking it up in its mouth and returning it obediently.

With proper training, it is possible to teach any young Sheltie the art of retrieving. Throw a suitably sized, nonedible ball or stick, with your dog standing next to you, and call out "Fetch." Provided that you did not throw the object clear out of the dog's sight, it will most likely run after it.

If the dog picks up the object in its mouth and returns to you, command the dog to sit, put out your hand, palm up, under its lower jaw, and say, "Let go!" You should be able to remove the object from the dog's mouth without any resistance. If your dog drops the object, place it back into its mouth, and then remove it, saying "Let go!"

If your Sheltie shows no desire to return with the object, repeat the exercise using a 30–foot (9 m) rope. Tie the dog to the cord, throw the object, and call out "Fetch!" again. Once it has picked up the object, draw the dog toward you. Then take the object from the dog.

If your dog hesitates in picking up the object, then place the object in its mouth and follow the commands for relinquishing an object. Keep repeating this lesson until the dog understands that this object is to be taken into its mouth. Then throw

Basic and Advanced Training

the object only a short distance to see if the dog will pick it up.

With patience and persistence you can teach your Sheltie to perform this command as well as if it were a retriever bringing a hunter its prey.

Jumping Over Hurdles

This may not be as difficult a lesson as you may think (provided the hurdles are Sheltie–sized). Herding dogs must know how to jump over obstacles if need be, to prevent a flock from scattering, and you may find that your dog will learn this lesson with relative ease. First, command your dog to sit on one side of a small pile of boards, while you stand on the opposite side. Command the dog by saying, "Jump!" If it walks around the obstacle, say "No!" then bring it back and start over. Praise your dog for a successful performance.

As your dog learns to jump over the hurdle on command, gradually increase the obstacle's height. Be careful not to make the jump too high, for this can hurt young dogs and discourage further jumping.

Once your dog has learned to jump on command, begin a jump and retrieve exercise. Place the object to be retrieved on the other side of the hurdle. Command your dog to sit next to you. Then command it to retrieve the object by saying, "Jump! Fetch!" in a clear, firm voice. The dog should leap over the obstacle, pick up the object, and jump back with it. Tell the dog to sit again. Then take the object out of its mouth by saying, "Let go!" Praise your dog warmly for its accomplishments.

Problems in Training

No two Shetland sheepdogs are precisely alike. Each has its own idiosyncrasies, and individual learning abilities can vary greatly. The key in training is to establish the proper rapport with your dog. As I have stated earlier, the training exercises described in this book are merely outlines for teaching commands. It is your responsibility, as your dog's trainer, to establish an effective system of communication. This will make it easier for your Sheltie to understand your commands and perform them well.

If you reach a point when your Sheltie has trouble learning a lesson, remain patient and understanding. Never try to force your Sheltie to learn. Anger and beating have never helped a dog learn anything! They only serve to create an atmosphere that is not conducive to learning. Eventually this will cause your Sheltie to lose trust in you.

When you and your pupil hit a roadblock, start by examining your teaching methods. Review the seven basic rules of training (page 59), and correct any mistakes that you may have been making. In most cases you will find that your teaching method was causing the problem.

If, after thoroughly reviewing your methods, you feel that this is not the problem, carefully examine your dog and its environment. Your Sheltie could possibly be distracted by an outside factor. If so, then you must remove the distraction. Could your dog be ill? If illness is suspected, make an appointment to see your veterinarian.

Should you continue to run into training difficulties, I strongly recommend that you contact a reputable obedience school. In many instances, the human ego will not allow us to believe that we could be doing anything wrong. Professional dog handlers who run these training facilities can usually spot problems rather easily.

By starting early and working hard, you will most assuredly be able to train your Sheltie to whatever stage you desire. Only as you grow older with your Sheltie will you begin to understand the importance of proper training, and begin to reap its rewards. Through diligence and the establishment of a harmonious training atmosphere, you and your faithful four–legged companion will enjoy many wonderful years of camaraderie.

Understanding Shelties

Origins and Early History

Although the Shetland sheepdog clearly has older roots, the first clear records of its existence date back to the early 1800s. At about this time, visitors to the Shetland Islands brought back to the mainland of England and Scotland small farm dogs called "toonies." These toonies that were being used to care for sheep in the Shetlands were described as a small breed of collie. Using this description, there is little doubt that the toonies were what we now call Shetland sheepdogs.

Today's Sheltie is a direct descendant of the small sheepherding dog used in the northern islands of Scotland. The harsh climate and rough terrain of the islands do not make them the ideal location to raise an abundance of large cattle. Vegetation is sparse on these islands and there are few places to hide from the severe North Sea storms that frequent the island. With limited food sources and space requirements, it would be almost impossible for large species of cattle, or any other large land animal, to long survive in the Shetlands.

Luckily, nature has a way of solving its own problems. In order for animals to survive in the Shetland Islands, they had to be adaptable. Smaller, hardier animals could survive in this harsh environment, for they require less food and can find shelter in many more places than can larger animals. So, after generation upon generation of evolution, literally all of the animals common to the Shetland Islands have become smaller and hardier than their cousins on the mainland. This reduction in size can be seen in both the domestic and wild animals that inhabit the islands. Besides the Shetland sheepdog, one of the best known examples of this is the Shetland pony. Like the diminutiveness of the Sheltie, the small size of the Shetland pony is very much a result of the Islands' environment.

The rugged landscape and severe weather of the Islands rule out commercial farming, while the isolated location of the Shetlands make them an impractical place to establish many factories. It is therefore logical that for a long time the raising of livestock has been the major industry of the Shetland Islands.

The types of livestock that can be raised effectively on the Shetland Islands must be able to adapt to the terrain and climate. After generations of raising livestock on the Islands, the domestic cattle and sheep evolved into miniature versions of their mainland predecessors.

While the exact origins of the Shetland sheepdog are unknown, it is generally believed that it is the descendant of a small working dog that was also the progenitor of the modern show collie.

Accentuating the effects of the island environment is the fact that the small working dog was also crossed with other small breeds believed to have been residing in, or indigenous to, the Islands.

It is not known how long it took to complete the evolution of the modern–day Shetland sheepdog, for there are no written records. Because these dogs were bred in the relative isolation of the Islands, it took a long time before the breed became known to the dog enthusiasts of the outside world. Thus, it was not until 1909 that the Sheltie obtained its initial recognition by the English Kennel Club when it was classified as a Shetland collie. In 1914 the breed obtained a separate classification and has since been known as the Shetland sheepdog. In 1915 the first Challenge Certificate was awarded to the breed.

Over the years several Shetland sheepdog clubs have been formed. Unfortunately, their history has always been one of controversy over variations in the acceptable size and type of the breed. The oldest club, the Shetland Sheepdog Club of the Islands, was founded in 1908. Their standard asked for a "rough collie in miniature" with a height not to exceed 15 inches (38 cm). The Scottish Shetland Sheepdog Club, founded in 1909, at first requested an "ordinary collie in miniature," with an ideal height of 12 inches (30 cm). Later this Club changed its standard to read "a modern show collie in miniature," and changed the dog's ideal height to 13½ inches (34 cm). The English Shetland Sheepdog

Club, an offshoot of the Scottish Club, was founded in 1914, and like its parent club, its members also had their own opinion as to the ideal Sheltie. The English Club called for "approximately a show collie in miniature" with an ideal height of 12 inches (30 cm), which was later changed to an acceptable range of 12 to 15 inches (30–38 cm) the ideal being 13½ inches (34 cm). Adding to the controversy was the British Breeders Association, which was an offspring of the English Club. They called for "a show collie in miniature" while maintaining the same heights as their parent club.

Finally in 1930, both the Scottish and English Clubs revised their standards to read "should resemble a collie (rough) in miniature." Even today, some variations still exist among the different clubs in the British Isles; however, these differences are now in a much more refined form.

The different standards among the various clubs were a reflection of the breeders' struggle to obtain and perpetuate the ideal size and type. As mentioned, the progenitor working collie was bred to other smaller breeds in order to reduce its size. The crossbreeding risked introducing characteristics contradictory to the true collie type. Crossbreeding the working collie with small spaniels, for instance, resulted in undesirable traits such as wavy coats, houndlike ears, long bodies, large round eyes, and wagging tails. On the other hand, these spaniels also brought the beneficial characteristics of calm and devoted dispositions. It is also believed that a little yellow dog from Iceland that had a dark muzzle and pricked ears also influenced the breed.

To counteract the undesirable traits that were beginning to appear, crosses with modern collies were made. This cross was responsible for improving the head properties, such as ear type and expression, as well as enabling the breeder to obtain the beautiful, weather-resistant coat. However, even this crossbreeding had its faults, such as legginess, excessive size, loss of substance, and imbalance.

Thus, it was up to the breeder to breed these new smaller collies in such a way as to produce a dog having all the traits associated with a correct collie, while at the same time attempting to keep the correct balance and size that we associate with our modern-day Sheltie.

The Shetland Sheepdog Standard that is presently approved by the Kennel Club of Great Britain has essentially the same requirements set forth by the AKC. If you plan to register your Sheltie in England or show your dog internationally, it would be wise to obtain a copy of the British Standard.

The major difference between the Standards of Kennel Club of Great Britain and AKC lies once again in the Sheltie's height. The British Standard states that the ideal height for Shelties is 14½ inches (37 cm) for males and 14 inches (35.5 cm) for females. The American Kennel Club Standard calls for a height of between 13 and 16 inches (32.5–40 cm) at the shoulder. Any height measurement over one inch (2.5 cm) above the ideal is to be considered a serious fault.

The Shetland Sheepdog in the United States

While there are records of the Sheltie brought to New York in 1911, it was not until 1929 that the American Shetland Sheepdog Association (ASSA) was formed. When developing the Shetland Sheepdog Standard for AKC approval, the ASSA combined the best of all of the British Standards. As stated, the current AKC–approved standard specifies a height from 13 to 16 inches (32.5–40 cm).

The first Sheltie breeders in the United States encountered problems like those in the British Isles. In their attempts to improve the physical characteristics of the breed, the American Shelties were crossed with their larger cousins, the show collie. In order to maintain the small size associated with the Sheltie, crosses only with smaller collies were made. However, like in Great Britain, this practice resulted in oversized dogs.

Since then, improvement of the Shetland sheepdog has been done only through selective breeding. Now the common practice is to breed Shelties that have some weaker traits with dogs of the same breed that are stronger in the targeted physical or behavioral characteristics. As a result, the modern show Shetland sheepdog has become a beautifully balanced dog that has the type, weather–resistant coat, and expression of a collie combined with the Sheltie's smaller size, character, and charm.

The Nature of the Shetland Sheepdog

Now that we have examined the origins of the Sheltie, you see how it acquired its size, shape, and color. To understand the Sheltie's behavior patterns, however, we must examine the process by which dogs evolved and were domesticated. All dogs, regardless of breed, trace their ancestry to a form of wild dog or wolf.

Wild dogs have a specially structured society. Most of their behavior rituals allow each member of the pack to live in harmony with the others. With the passing of countless generations of dogs, some of these rituals became instinctive. Modern domesticated dogs exhibit many of these instinctive behavior patterns, including marking of territory and establishing a ranking order among human companions.

It is believed that dogs were the first domesticated animal; evidence indicates that this process began about 12,000 years ago. Humans probably tamed wolves or wild dogs to assist them in hunting. Hunting practices and social structures of both humans and dogs were probably very similar at this time.

As dogs became domestic, they lost many of their instinctive behavior patterns but retained some. Which traits were lost and which were retained depends on the specific breed and how it was domesticated. As you know, Shetland sheepdogs were originally bred as herding dogs, as were most of their domestic ancestors. Thus, Shelties naturally display excellent herding and watchdog skills. While it is true that not all of our modern Shelties exhibit all the skills necessary to be an effective herding dog, many of these traits have become part of this breed's instinctive behavioral pattern. An example of this can be seen in the natural movements and temperament of the Sheltie. The physical structure of the Sheltie enables the dog to exhibit strength, speed, grace, and jumping power—all necessary attributes for the successful herding dog. Shelties are also instinctively loyal and affectionate to their owners, while showing reserve, but not nervousness, to strangers. All of these traits, with the addition of the Sheltie's alertness, are common to all Shetland sheepdogs, yet these features are not seen in all breeds of dogs.

Because Shelties and their domestic ancestors were herding dogs, they experienced considerable human contact. Dogs used as sheepdogs must undergo substantial training by a shepherd. This relationship makes the dog into a companion to the shepherd, not just a herding tool. More than any other factor, the generations of the shepherd/sheepdog relationship are responsible for the vigilant, obedient, protective, and easy–to–train nature of the Sheltie.

Most of the physical attributes of the Shetland sheepdog are the result of generations of selective breeding. During the last century, breeders have also carefully developed the temperament they deemed desirable in sheepdogs and have tried to eliminate unwanted behavioral problems. For instance, it would be undesirable to have an aggressive sheepdog. This would frighten the sheep just as much as any predator they might encounter. Therefore, a Sheltie breeder would avoid mating any dogs that are considered aggressive. Thus, breeders have successfully weeded out many inherent canine behaviors that would be undesirable in a herding dog.

In summary, the nature of the Shetland sheepdog is a blend of three elements. The first includes all instinctive behavior, such as sexual drive, the marking of territories, and the establishment of a ranking order. The second and third elements are a result of domestication; they include selectively bred traits and "people–oriented" traits developed from the shepherd–dog relationship.

Behavior Problems

Because of the care and consistency used by Shetland sheepdog breeders, there are relatively few behavior problems encountered in this breed. In recent years, however, as the popularity of the Sheltie increases, we can also see an increase in poorly bred dogs. These dogs have been mated by unscrupulous breeders who have obtained the cheapest stud dogs, who care little for the advancement of the breed, and are doing this only to make a profit. Poor breeding practices usually result in dogs that, besides not meeting the physical requirements of the Standard, have behavior problems. These problems include shyness, overaggressiveness, or hyperactivity, to name a few.

The major behavior problem associated with the Sheltie is shyness. Although some may not consider shyness in a dog a problem, you must remember that Shelties are herding dogs, and it would be ludicrous to put a timid dog out in the fields to protect your flock.

Shyness, however, is not a new problem to the Sheltie breeder; in fact, it dates back to when the dogs were first discovered in the Shetland Islands. It is believed that in the isolation of the Islands, Shelties rarely encountered humans beside their owners. It was found that these dogs reacted in one of two ways: they were either cautious and watchful of strangers; or they became timid and moved away. So from early in their history, Sheltie breeders have encountered the unwanted trait of excessive timidity.

As a general practice, quality breeders have avoided breeding shy Shelties, and this problem has always been under control. However, because there are breeders ready to compromise for profit, an increase in shy Shetland sheepdogs has been seen along with the increase of the breed's popularity.

While it may be possible to detect some shyness in a Sheltie puppy, many times the extent of this problem cannot be seen until the dog is older. Therefore, be sure to purchase your dog from a reliable and conscientious breeder. Even if you do this, however, your dog may still develop behavior problems. Sometimes it is possible to control this problem through extensive training and counter-conditioning. If, however, you do find that your Sheltie has any problems, be it shyness, overaggressiveness, or any other abnormal behavior, do not mate your dog. While your dog still may be a loved one to you, it is best for the sake of the breed not to increase the incidence of these problems.

What Your Dog Can Tell You

All dogs use their voices, body language, and facial expressions to convey their emotions. You must pay special attention to these signals to understand your dog's moods.

Dogs do not make noises without a reason. Each sound reflects a mood. A dog will yelp in fright or pain, whine and whimper in loneliness or when seeking attention, groan in contentment or when ailing, and bark in anger or glee. Often you must look for additional signs to determine the purpose of the sounds.

Body language is also a good indicator of a dog's mood. A joyous dog jumps up and down eagerly and may bark. A dog that crouches and lowers its head to the floor is exhibiting fear, either of being punished, or of an intruder, or another dog. The

Understanding Shelties

best indicator of your dog's emotions, however, is its tail. A happy dog wags its tail briskly; the happier it is, the more briskly its tail wags. A frightened dog puts its tail between its legs. An alert or attentive Sheltie raises its tail slightly, while a contented dog has a lowered tail (but not between its legs).

Finally, watch your Sheltie's ears and muzzle, for they are a primary means of facial expression. A contented Sheltie has a closed mouth and normal set ears. An alert, aroused, or attentive dog picks up its ears. Often your dog will cock its head inquisitively to one side or the other. Be wary of *any* dog whose ears are back, upper lips are raised, mouth is open, and is growling. Although you will rarely see a Sheltie in this position, remember that these are all warning signals of fear and/or anger, and they may precede an attack.

The Sense Organs

Dogs in general rely heavily on the senses of smell, hearing, taste, and touch, and less on the sense of sight. Like other features, sense organs in a particular breed have been developed through selective breeding and domestication.

The sense of smell is very important to a Sheltie. This sense enables it to find food, locate a mate, and decipher territories.

The area of the olfactory system concerned with smell is more than 40 times larger in a Sheltie than in humans; in addition, Shelties can remember thousands of odors and can associate them with the appropriate people, animals, and places.

Shelties also possess a highly developed sense of hearing, superior to that of humans. They hear a wider range of sounds, especially high–pitched frequencies, such as those emitted from a Galton whistle ("silent" dog whistle). Shelties hear sounds from a much greater distance than do humans. Their acute hearing is also important to their usefulness as herding dogs. Many shepherds train their dogs to perform commands at the sound of various whistle codes. They do this because high-pitched

whistle sounds can travel farther, and even during stormy weather can be heard more clearly by the sheepdog.

Shelties' peripheral vision is much greater than that of humans; however, their eyes do not focus as sharply as do those of humans. As a result, their eyes are much more sensitive to motion, but they must rely more on smell and sound to interpret what they see.

Because Shelties possess a long, thick, two–layered, weather–resistant coat, their bodies may appear to lack some sensitivity. However, the body parts that are not covered by this thick coat, such as the muzzle and nose, do seem to have a high degree of feeling.

Like other dogs, Shelties possess other senses that we still do not understand completely. For example, they have an innate sense of navigation. We have all heard reports of dogs traveling hundreds of miles to return home.

As Your Puppy Grows Older

Additional insight into your Sheltie can be gained when you examine the dog's aging process. As your dog goes through the various stages of its life it will be undergoing both physical and emotional changes. The first major change will occur when the young puppy is removed from its littermates and placed into what is expected to become its permanent home.

From the time a puppy is born until it is in its seventh week, it leads a quiet and secure life in the presence of its mother, brothers, and sisters. At the point when the puppy is relocated in its new home, it is becoming much more aware of the world around it. A puppy at this age is very curious, mischievous, and also very impressionable. Training serves as a method of satisfying its curiosity and enables the puppy to learn the rules of its new home. Training will also help the puppy differentiate between playtime and serious time.

Around this time in a puppy's life it is also becoming more aware of its own physical attributes. Even before you bring your puppy home, it will have already begun to have mock fights with its littermates. This serves to build up strength and to improve motor skills.

When you bring your puppy home, you will find that it is both emotionally and physically ready to adapt itself to its new household. Thus, training should begin immediately. If you wait too long, you will allow this impressionable little creature to pick up bad habits, some of which you may never up-root.

By the time your puppy is 12 or 13 weeks old, it reaches what I refer to as "the questioning stage." The questioning stage for a puppy is similar to that point when a human child asks "Why is the sky blue?", shortly followed by "Why this?" and "Why that?" In your puppy's case, it has become completely aware of itself and its environment. Its favorite pastime will be to share its discoveries with you. It will begin to investigate everything, primarily with its teeth, for at this time it begins to lose its baby teeth and get its permanent ones. Remember that your puppy is still very impressionable, so treat it with care, and continue to reinforce the basic rules of your house.

At seven to ten months old your puppy will have reached almost its full adult size. This is also when the dog reaches sexual maturity, the equivalent of human adolescence. Its once innocent curiosity will have changed into a bold and assertive interest. This is also a time when, as a teenager might do, your dog begins to test the system. At this point your Sheltie should be much more comfortable with your lifestyle, and will feel it should be included in all your activities. Your Sheltie should know exactly what you expect of it, and how it should behave. However, it will naturally try to challenge you in order to improve its rank. This is, after all, a part of its instinctive canine behavior. When this happens, do not lose your temper. Just teach your Sheltie calmly and firmly that you are the authority. In doing this you can lead your dog through its final stage of development.

Once your Sheltie reaches maturity, it probably will not undergo any behavioral changes (with the exception of mating urges) until it reaches a ripe old age. Your consistency and evenness of temper in training your dog should now pay off with many years of companionship with a loving, devoted, and trustworthy Shetland sheepdog.

Changes that occur in the geriatric years are more dependent on the individual dog and on its medical background. With many "old" dogs, changes in their daily routines or behavior are often due to a medical problem brought on by old age. As your dog ages, its digestive and immune systems begin slowly to deteriorate. The long–term results can include circulatory, musculoskeletal, and nervous system problems. Thus, your older dog might become lethargic or moody, lose its orientation, or experience hearing loss; it may even forget learned responses. This all may sound dreadful, but it is simply a part of the aging process, and there is not much you can do except try to understand.

Encounters in the Outside World

As part of its heritage as a sheepdog, it is important that a Sheltie learn not to fear people. It is normal for a Sheltie to be wary of strangers, but a sheepdog should never display fear. You can help your dog overcome this problem by introducing it to the outside world and the ways of other humans while it is still very young. In addition to removing the feelings of fear, this will also help your dog learn to behave properly when you have visitors.

On occasion take your dog with you when you shop. Exposure to strange places and people (as long as you accompany it) will help increase the puppy's confidence in itself and in you. Also take the dog on short auto trips. Gradually lengthen the trips until the puppy is used to traveling. A familiarization with travel will make future vacations with your dog much more pleasant.

When you travel by car, keep your dog in a small

Understanding Shelties

cage to prevent it from getting in your way and to protect it from injury from sudden stops. When you leave your puppy in the car, always open the windows enough for proper ventilation, but not so much that the dog can jump out. Heat can build up in a car very rapidly, so always park in the shade. If you plan to be gone from the car a long time, leave your dog at home.

In order to truly familiarize your puppy with the ways of the world, walk it (on a leash) in areas where you are likely to encounter other humans and other dogs as well. Allow your puppy to have contact with other humans, as long as that person doesn't mind. It is important that, as the teacher, you show no hesitation toward an approaching stranger. Sometimes your dog can sense this hesitation and will interpret it as a reason to shy away.

When any two dogs encounter each other, it is inevitable that they will try to establish a ranking order. In most cases this is determined through a mock fight (usually looking like playful wrestling) whereby one dog ends up lying on its back in a subordinate position. However, if neither dog is willing to back down, a real fight might ensue, so be prepared for this possibility. If either dog displays a threatening posture or growls in anger, remove your dog immediately.

If you should encounter another dog, restrain your puppy until the strange dog approaches it. If the two dogs wag their tails and then sniff each others nose and tail, you can assume that they like each other. Encourage your Sheltie to play with the other dog. Playing will make your Sheltie feel more comfortable in strange surroundings. If you choose to let your Sheltie play, you can remove the leash, but remain nearby and alert in case you are needed.

Useful Addresses and Literature

International Kennel Clubs
American Shetland Sheepdog Association*
2516 Country Club Drive
Odessa, TX 79762
American Kennel Club
51 Madison Avenue
New York, NY 10038
Australian National Kennel Club
Royal Show Grounds
Ascot Vale
Victoria
Australia
Canadian Kennel Club
111 Eglington Avenue
Toronto 12, Ontario
Canada
The Kennel Club
1–4 Clargis Street
Picadilly
London, W7Y 8AB
England

* This address may change as a new officer is elected. The latest listing can always be obtained from the American Kennel Club.

Books

Alderton, David *The Dog Care Manual*. Barron's Educational Series, Hauppauge, New York, 1986.

Baer, Ted *Communicating with Your Dog*. Barron's Educational Series, Hauppauge, New York, 1984.

Frye, Fredric L. *First Aid for Your Dog*. Barron's Educational Series, Hauppauge, New York, 1987.

Klever, Ulrich *The Complete Book of Dog Care*. Barron's Educational Series, Hauppauge, New York, 1989.

Lorenz, Konrad Z. *Man Meets Dog*. Penguin Books, London and New York, 1967.

Ullman, Hans-J. *The New Dog Handbook*. Barron's Educational Series, Hauppauge, New York, 1984.

Touring with Towser: a directory of hotels and motels that accommodate guests with dogs. Gaines TWT, P.O. Box 8172, Kankakee, Illinois 60901 (price: $1.50).

Index

Index

Perfect for Pet Owners!

PET OWNER'S MANUALS

Over 50 illustrations per book
(20 or more color photos),
72-80 pp., paperback.

AFRICAN GRAY PARROTS (3773-1)
AMAZON PARROTS (4035-X)
BANTAMS (3687-5)
BEAGLES (3829-0)
BEEKEEPING (4089-9)
BOXERS (4036-8)
CANARIES (2614-4)
CATS (2421-4)
CHINCHILLAS (4037-6)
CHOW-CHOWS (3952-1)
COCKATIELS (2889-9)
COCKATOOS (4159-3)
DACHSHUNDS (2888-0)
DOBERMAN PINSCHERS (2999-2)
DWARF RABBITS (3669-7)
FEEDING AND SHELTERING
   BACKYARD BIRDS (4252-2)
FEEDING AND SHELTERING
   EUROPEAN BIRDS (2858-9)
FERRETS (2976-3)
GERBILS (3725-1)
GERMAN SHEPHERDS (2982-8)
GOLDEN RETRIEVERS (3793-6)
GOLDFISH (2975-5)
GUINEA PIGS (2629-2)
HAMSTERS (2422-2)
LABRADOR RETRIEVERS (3792-8)
LHASA APSOS (3950-5)
LIZARDS IN THE TERRARIUM
   (3925-4)
LONG-HAIRED CATS (2803-1)
LOVEBIRDS (3726-X)
MICE (2921-6)
MUTTS (4126-7)
MYNAS (3688-3)
PARAKEETS (2423-0)
PARROTS (2630-6)
PERSIAN CATS (4405-3)
PIGEONS (4044-9)
PONIES (2856-2)
POODLES (2812-0)
RABBITS (2615-2)

SCHNAUZERS (3949-1)
SHEEP (4091-0)
SHETLAND SHEEPDOGS (4264-6)
SIBERIAN HUSKIES (4265-4)
SNAKES (2813-9)
SPANIELS (2424-9)
TROPICAL FISH (2686-1)
TURTLES (2631-4)
YORKSHIRE TERRIERS (4406-1)
ZEBRA FINCHES (3497-X)

NEW PET HANDBOOKS

Detailed, illustrated profiles (40-60
color photos), 144 pp., paperback.

NEW AQUARIUM HANDBOOK
   (3682-4)
NEW BIRD HANDBOOK (4157-7)
NEW CAT HANDBOOK (2922-4)
NEW COCKATIEL HANDBOOK
   (4201-8)
NEW DOG HANDBOOK (2857-0)
NEW DUCK HANDBOOK (4088-0)
NEW FINCH HANDBOOK (2859-7)
NEW GOAT HANDBOOK (4090-2)
NEW PARAKEET HANDBOOK
   (2985-2)
NEW PARROT HANDBOOK (3729-4)
NEW RABBIT HANDBOOK (4202-6)
NEW SOFTBILL HANDBOOK
   (4075-9)
NEW TERRIER HANDBOOK
   (3951-3)

CAT FANCIER'S SERIES

Authoritative, colorful guides (over
35 color photos), 72 pp., paperback.
BURMESE CATS (2925-9)
LONGHAIR CATS (2923-2)

FIRST AID FOR PETS

Fully illustrated, colorful guide, 20 pp.,
Hardboard with hanging chain and
   index tabs.

FIRST AID FOR YOUR CAT (5827-5)
FIRST AID FOR YOUR DOG (5828-3)

REFERENCE BOOKS

Comprehensive, lavishly illustrated
references (60-300 color photos),
136-176 pp., hardcover & paperback

AQUARIUM FISH SURVIVAL
   MANUAL (5686-8), hardcover
AUSTRALIAN FINCHES, THE
   COMPLETE BOOK OF (6091-1),
   hardcover
BEST PET NAME BOOK EVER, THE
   (4258-1), paperback
CAT CARE MANUAL (5765-1),
   hardcover
COMMUNICATING WITH YOUR
   DOG (4203-4), paperback
COMPLETE BOOK OF
   BUDGERIGARS (6059-8),
   hardcover
COMPLETE BOOK OF PARROTS
   (5971-9), hardcover
DOG CARE, THE COMPLETE BOOK
   OF (4158-5), paperback
DOG CARE MANUAL (5764-3),
   hardcover
GOLDFISH AND ORNAMENTAL
   CARP (5634-5), hardcover
HORSE CARE MANUAL (5795-3),
   hardcover
LABYRINTH FISH (5635-3),
   hardcover
NONVENOMOUS SNAKES (5632-9),
   hardcover
WATER PLANTS IN THE AQUARIUM
   (3926-2), paperback

GENERAL GUIDE BOOKS

Heavily illustrated with color photos,
144 pp., paperback.

COMMUNICATING WITH YOUR DOG
   (4203-4)
DOGS (4158-5)

ISBN prefix: 0-8120

Order from your favorite book or pet store

Barron's Educational Series, Inc. • P.O. Box 8040, 250 Wireless Blvd., Hauppauge, NY 11788
Call toll-free: 1-800-645-3476, in NY: 1-800-257-5729 • In Canada: Georgetown Book Warehouse
34 Armstrong Ave., Georgetown, Ont. L7G 4R9 • Call toll-free: 1-800-668-4336